Smoke-Pot
Days

Smoke-Pot Days

by Will Jackson

Illustrations: Bendel Hydes

Cayman National Cultural Foundation
Grand Cayman, Cayman Islands

Cover painting: *Source #17* by Bendel Hydes. Collection: Oscar Balcon
Text illustrations – Bendel Hydes
Cover Design – Patrick Gorham
Book Design – Dave Martins

Published by Cayman National Cultural Foundation
        Box 30201SMB, West Bay Road, Grand Cayman, Cayman Islands.

To my wife, Sybil,
who
turned my life around

Moving to East End

CONTENTS

Introduction   1

Prologue   3

1.   Young Stirrings   4

2.   Teenage Years   17

3.   Changing Cayman   22

4.   Tragedies at Sea   29

5.   Moving Forward   36

6.   Then and Now   46

7.   Looking Backward   53

8.   The Rise Begins   63

9.   Mystery and Tragedy   78

10. From Thatch Roof to Spanish Tile   89

     Glossary   94

INTRODUCTION
by Oswell Rankine
Founding Chairman – Cayman National Cultural Foundation

Webster defines culture as "the concepts, habits, skills, instruments, art, institutions, etc. of a given people in a given period", and through the efforts of Mr. Percival Vibert "Will" Jackson, one of the highly respected and well-known men of our soil, this book gives us the opportunity to reflect on some of those aspects of our Islands in times past, and to gain more insights in self-knowledge. Here, in a concise but easily digestible form, the casual reader as well as the more academic interest both have an abundance of accurate information that has previously been neglected, or unknown, or both.

In his natural, narrative style of description, Mr. Will has captured the essence of what many senior citizens refer to as "the good old days" while retaining its cultural and historical importance. While this sentimental view may still be held by some, the author reminds us that those were also often difficult and even terrifying times.

To reflect on the family life, work ethic, neighbourliness, and accountability of that era is to see those aspects as the basic tenets of a small but progressive society in the making, but we should also take careful note of the numerous contrasts identified—including the negative side of our new-found and much touted affluence—as well as the tracing of the changing economic influences in the early years. Of particular import is the spotlighting of the true contributors to the initial development of our Islands—our seamen, including our veterans of foreign wars. For too long, we have largely ignored those contributions. Similar comments can be expressed regarding the developers of infrastructure, particularly the opening of roads, and the visionary outlook of the British Commissioner Cardinall.

In the long term, *Smoke-Pot Days* will become an important resource, pointing our writers, historians, and educators toward subjects and personalities worthy of closer examination. In that light, this book will continue to exert a subtle but positive influence among us far beyond its patent immediate ability to surprise and delight.

Will Jackson

PROLOGUE

Unlike the case today, life in these Cayman Islands for more than a hundred years, was most strenuous indeed as the natives lived in a hand-to-mouth fashion, from one day into the next. Nonetheless, they were content with their existence, braving the hardships, difficulties and privations that attended their ways in founding a country for themselves. The people grew their own provisions and fruits, tended cows, and sustained themselves from the sea in one way or another.

Those early settlers seem to have been primarily of English and Scottish descent—such names as Scott, and Banks; Bouden, Borden or Bodden; McCoy, McLaughlin, McLean and Jackson; then there were the Edens and Smiths, just to name a few—and, of course, a goodly number of black slaves.

According to my grandfather, Simpson Jackson, wherever they came from to establish residence in these Islands they were persons of high repute. As for tales of pirate ancestors, he would scoff, "Pirates? No sir. They were all good Christians." From the very early days Caymanians have enjoyed a history of peace, and a law-abiding disposition. There are no recorded revolutions or uprisings throughout 200 and more years of settlement.

I am a "true-born Caymanian", born to full-blooded Caymanians in the old Cayman dispensation, and I have experienced my share of problems and trials in my 70 years—at the age of three I lost my mother; my father was a seaman, and was away from home for months at a time; my maternal grandparents both were found dead on their farm on my eighth birthday; a kind old lady struck me down out of her tamarind tree at the age of nine and smashed my collar-bone; I was rescued on the open sea when my ship went down in a storm.

In my youth, there was little of material worth in these Islands. There was no money to spend, no jobs from which to choose, no prospects were waiting. A machete was the major tool of trade during those hard old days, and the country men, those who were not lucky enough to get on a fishing boat, had to travel to town and use their machete, clearing cow pastures under most dire conditions, for weeks at a time, for small pay.

There were always swarms of mosquitoes, nests of ticks, and pods of cowitch waiting to greet the poor country boys whose ambition was strong enough to better the cashless condition that prevailed.

For a long time, we lagged behind the progress that was taking place in other parts of the West Indies. Even in an Island as small as Grand Cayman, the shortage of roads made life very difficult, to the extent that many people spent their entire lives without ever going outside the borders of the district in which they had been born.

Well, we have come from under thatch-roof to Spanish tile; out of white lime plaster to cement block wall; from living behind stuffy wooden doors and windows to looking out through graceful glass windows and louvre doors; walking away from the old, hard pine floor, lightly treading on ankle-deep carpets and Persian rugs—this is a picture of yesterday's living quarters contrasted against today's luxurious houses.

We have truly received numerous blessings and have come a far way, but there are many things about those bygone days that many old-timers continue to yearn for because while we have made great changes and gained great affluence it is also true that we have lost the sense of community and family we once knew. This book deals in part with my sea life of 22 years and mainly with my reminiscences of that early Cayman that, for the most part, is no more.

P.V. Jackson

1

EARLY
STIRRINGS

My maternal grandparents, Thomas Welcome and his wife Matilda, make quite a sensational story for my readers, to which I will come later on. My mother, I have been told, was beautiful. She was the youngest daughter of the late Thomas and Matilda Welcome, my father was the great-grandson of the early settler Sharer Jackson who inhabited the Newlands area and owned slaves.

In the first place no one seemed to have known just what my name might have been. From my earliest remembrance they called me 'Will'. During my school days, officially I began to be called, 'Wilbert'. Then later I was 'Wilber'; but my relatives still called me 'Will'. I have no remembrance of my dear mother. I was two-and-a-half-years old when she died, and of that I did not spend more than the half of that time with her where she lived because she was having her second baby and was not well.

My father and my mother were married in the year 1919, but I did not come along until 1922. My father was a seaman who travelled a lot, and stayed away for long periods at a time—Nicaragua and Panama, during those days were like the U.S.A of today—and sometimes two years might have gone by without him reaching home. Well, it so happened that before I became a year old another baby was growing; however, my dear little sister died just a few months before my mother in 1925. So it was, at the tender age of 15 months I was given over to the care of my father's sister and my grandfather, Simpson Jackson. You talk about lavished love; well, I had it thrown on me. In those days pity was indeed shown to the orphans and the bereaved. Dear little 'Will' was everybody's darling. My dear Aunt Florrie was then unmarried and had no child of her own, so

I became her everything. Then there was my dear grandfather Simpson; his wife, my grandmother, died when I hardly knew her, so Grandpa lavished all his love and affection on his motherless grandson. Following the deaths of my mother and sister, my father remained in Central and South America for a couple of years before he returned home. It must have been an awfully hard homecoming for Dad to face the absence of his beloved wife and baby daughter all at one time.

My first recollection of knowing my father was not very exciting for me, because I had gotten to know and love only Aunt Florrie as my mother, and grandfather was the dearest person on earth to me, but then this huge giant of a man was about to squeeze his way into my daily living, although I sometimes don't think that my father cared so much about me in those early days. His deepest thoughts, while at home, were on the dead rather than the living. I remember a couple of men struggling, fighting as it were, with Dad one day during that first Christmas he spent at home; they were trying to disarm him of a gun, a .32 automatic, with which he was about to shoot himself. Well, that gun was discharged twice during the hassle and left a bullet hole through the brim of his felt hat, barely burning his forehead. For many years, Grandpa kept that hat in his possession as a reminder of a near tragedy. Anyway in just a couple of weeks, Dad was off again, back to Panama; thus I didn't have to share my parental devotion.

When I was five years of age I was sent to a private school where I remained for two years. When I was seven, I promptly started into Government school, and I'll not soon forget my first day there because I became involved in the one rash act of my young life which led to my teacher flogging me like I had never been flogged before. Teacher Allen McLaughlin expressed deep regrets at having to whip me, but he only did his duty. It had never been like me to hurt anybody, but because another boy said, "Let's trip that girl down with this snare" I took part with him, and the dear little girl suffered skinned elbows and knees which had to be treated by the teacher's sister who was a registered nurse and lived next door. That pained me a lot more than any flogging ever could. The young girl was much older than I, but she became a life-long personal friend; after begging her pardon and forgiveness, we were close friends right up to her recent death.

In light of that experience, I recall that an old relative once taught me a gem to remember. It went:

"Dogs delight to bark and fight, for God has made them so.
Tigers, they will tear and bite for that's their nature to.
But children, they should never let such angry passion rise;
God delights to have them love and with each other always smile."

I had always been the standoffish one. I never easily made friends among the children, but was rather treated as the poor little motherless kid, which I deeply resented with a somewhat inferior feeling. I think I always suffered from an inferiority complex. It seems to me like books must have always been my best friend. I was always a bright student in school. While the other children played recess and lunch hour through, usually I took time to study. So I never failed an examination during my years at school. When I had spent two years in Standard Six, hoping to study for the Jamaica 3rd year, the family had no money for the necessary books, and I had to leave school to go to work. Nevertheless, my school days were not all pleasurable ones, or always smooth sailings. I had just about every children's disease that came around, including typhoid fever.

One episode that affected me for my entire life came from my love for tamarinds which drew me to Mrs. Marjorie Pat's tree, famous for its tasty fruit. She lived in the centre of East End, near where the Holiness Church is now. As school children, we would pass the tree on our way to and from school, and those tamarinds sure were tempting, but I kept heeding my grandfather's warnings not to interfere with what belonged to others. However, this day, my favourite little girl-friend asked me to get her some tamarinds and, grandfather's advice or not, up I went. I didn't see Miss Marjorie around, but I realised something was up when the other children started to run. Turns out the lady was hiding in the bush across the road looking for tamarind thieves. Well, she rushed out with this old striker— that's a long pointed stick the fisherman used to spear conch—and she started poking at me. I was up about 12 feet but she could still reach me, so I decided to jump down and land on her. I missed her, landed flush on my shoulder, and broke my collar-bone. Teacher Allen McLaughlin did first aid on me, but that shoulder mended badly and for many years after

8

The Tamarind Thief

my right arm was affected. I couldn't raise my hand to my mouth, I couldn't swim, I couldn't dive, and after I started to go to sea it got very bad—it became like a big raised ball. Eventually I had it operated on in New York in 1965; they took out 12 ounces of knotted matter and reset it, and it's been fine since. Miss Marjorie was a crusty old soul. The day of the accident, Justice of the Peace Mr. Austin Conolly told her I had been injured and they might prosecute her. She told him, "One of them git his collar bone broke; the next one will git his ass bone broke."

During those days of schooling, my father and I had become closely attached to each other. By 1930 he had gotten married again, and had brought his bride home to live in East End, but he continued to go to sea on local schooners. He was a great cook of his time, and his service was always in demand, so he was never beached for many weeks at a stretch.

We had several acres of good land which were cultivated into cow pastures, so we started rearing cows. Soon I found myself penning calves in the evening and milking cows in the morning before school. I became conditioned to hard work from very early in life. Always a lone rider, I never was afraid of hard work. Just past my 14th birthday I became initiated in the labour force as a youth. My standard of education was not all I desired or would have loved to obtain, but at least I had enough to take me over the testing high points of life. I could read anything written in the English language. I could write very well, and figure the last farthing.

■

In 1931, the only mother I knew, my Aunt Florrie, got married and went to live far away from the old homestead, leaving my grandfather and myself alone. By then my father had taken another wife, Christenell, but I did not know her, and, as a child sometimes reacts, I didn't think much of my step-mother then. I saw her as a proud and high-up person, not at all on my level. Of course I grew to love her, while she adored me. We became as close as any mother and son would be. She depended on me to do everything in my father's absence—he never really stayed home for many weeks at a time between voyages—such as taking care of the cows, the cultivations, fishing and so on. I was an underage little man.

We were living then in the old Cayman times. Conditions were almost primitive, but personally we fared off well. We always had lots of local produce, and Dad always brought home a lot of goodies from his trips abroad, whether Tampa, Panama, Jamaica or whenever he went. There always seemed to have been some cash to spend.

On 12 December 1930, on my eighth birthday, tragedy unveiled itself in the family ... that terrible day my Grandfather and Grandmother, Thomas and Matilda Welcome, were found dead on their farm. That was an event never to be forgotten. Even though I had not been closely associated with my maternal grandparents, I know they loved me dearly. Even now I sometimes think of what love they must have had for each other. Grandma was already dead when Grandpa found her, and because he could not manage to carry her from where she was he chose to lie down alongside her and die of grief and exposure. A later chapter will detail this tragic story further.

In contrast to that sad event in the Bluff Bay interior (that's the area east of Morritt's Tortuga), shortly after there was a windfall for the Cayman communities right out there on the Bluff Bay reef when a large three-masted ship went aground, deeply laden with lumbers which was close to gold for Caymanians. Captain Erskine Conolly of East End was the master of the *Halifax*, while his son Arnold was the chief mate. So no one need ask how or why was the ship grounded on Bluff Bay reef. That was the greatest blessing an individual had ever brought to Cayman; little lumber houses soon sprang up everywhere across the land.

Nevertheless that great blessing was soon enough changed into disaster, as in November 1932 the hurricane of the century swept over the land destroying everything in its path. Not only was Grand Cayman devastated in the '32 storm, but Cayman Brac suffered even more, as more than 100 lives were cut off in one day. I was then almost 10 years of age and have very sharp remembrances of the experience with the weather. Dad just happened to be at home then. He was building a modern house at the time, which was being made of concrete walls and zinc roofing. That house was being built so strong that even that great hurricane failed to damage it, even in its unfinished state. Many houses were destroyed or badly damaged. The 1932 storm marked the cause of the worst food shortage ever witnessed in the islands. That was the only time in my 73 years I know of Caymanians living on rationed hand-outs. By early 1933 there was indeed a famine throughout the land. There was almost nothing left around the cultivations to be had because what hadn't been destroyed by the storm was by then rotted. To survive, people were reduced to eating bulrush. Now bulrush, for the benefit of those who don't know, is a grassy bush that grows wild, primarily in cultivated lands. It might grow heads up to 20 pounds or more, and it contains a lot of nutritious starch which was great to feed babies with. The heads were chopped in pieces, peeled and grated. It then was washed out in water and strained through a porous cloth into a large container. The liquid then was left to settle overnight. The following day the water was poured off leaving all the starch settled in the container. It was then placed in the sun to dry out before being stowed away as food. This made a wonderful porridge cooked in coconut milk. Apart from the babies, it was also great for the sick and infirm. The meal, or trash, as some called it, was then made into balls and dried in the sun. When being used, it was beaten in a mortar and sifted. From that, cakes and dumplings were made. Cooked in the fish stew it was a savior to many families during lean times but never more so than after the '32 storm.

Anyway, looking back to my own personal experience ... early in 1933 my father decided to move to George Town for a while for more reasons than one. First, he had a brother living there who invited him to come down and work with him. Uncle Javis Jackson was a painter and artist. Right after the severe beating the town had taken in the storm there were many paint jobs waiting to be done. Second, Dad was a classed fisherman and trapper, and he owned a big catboat which he would take along with him. Then there was the wreck of the *Balboa* that still oozed pickings to be salvaged, so on the over all it was better in town.

For about three months we remained in town, my stepmother and I, and then, even though Dad was doing very well financially, he decided to go back to sea, so my stepmother and I made our way back home to the country to pick up the pieces and start all over again. In town I had gotten many new experiences. I had seen many things for the first time. I saw my first motor car, and first bicycle. The first electric light I had seen was there. There I ate ice cream for the first time. Now the fun was over. How I would have loved to just live in town, but we had nothing there; the country was our home and there we were bound. I must relate that home bound trip which was somewhat like making one's way far into the jungle away from civilization.

Going from George Town to East End was not a pleasurable trip with all our luggage. Mr. Logan Bodden, who owned a truck, took us and all our belongings to Bodden Town where we spent the night with relatives and laid plans with an old gentleman to take us to Frank Sound the next morning in an old leaky canoe, which I bailed the whole way, while the old man pushed it along with a long stick called a spreet.

The trip started just as the day began to dawn over Bodden Town, and we reached Frank Sound when the eastern sun was well up in the sky. At Breakers Point, where the reef closed in to the shoreline, it was rough, and the old man had to walk the canoe across; we were soaked by the breaking waves before we finally made it clear to the smooth water. We stopped at Mrs. Tama Jackson's house, the last house between Bodden Town and East End. There we left the greater part of our luggage and loaded ourselves with as much as we could carry. We then had to make our way to East End on foot, over some unpleasant terrain. The path was along the beach for more than a mile, and then through a foot-path with rough and uneven surfaces. We finally made it home by noon time, tired and exhausted, but happy to be back home. The next morning it was my task to take the donkey back to Frank Sound and load on the remainder of our belongings. Remember, this was 1933 and I wasn't 11 years old yet but doing a man's job.

There was much to be done at home, the yard was all grown over. The cultivations were all choked with bush, and, in the days following, my stepmother and I worked like slaves getting things organised because on Monday it would be back to school for me. I had missed a lot in three months, but I had not failed to study in town. As I look back on it, Dad had gone to Panama, but he had left a very industrious wife and a tough son at home.

2

TEENAGE
YEARS

*A*s far back as my remembrance will take me, I had been taught about Heaven and God. My Aunt Florrie was a very godly woman and she tried to let everybody know whom she loved. No one asked me if I would like to go to Sunday school on Sunday mornings. I just had to go unless I was sick in bed. Neither was I allowed to go home before church service was over. I was not allowed to go swimming, or out playing either on Sunday. My grandfather at that time was not a professed Christian, but was a proper good Sunday-terian. (A Sunday-terian was the kind of Christian who held Sunday in high esteem but on Monday he'd cuss you blind.) However, in later years he became a good old Christian. My stepmother, when I came to know her, was a staunch Seventh Day Adventist, but she never pressed her religion on me. I was a Presbyterian Sunday School kid, and loved to go there.

While residing in town in 1933 my father had been converted in the Church of God, then called Uncle Jimmy's Church, or the Arch's Church. But there was no branch of that church in East End, so in 1934 when Dad returned from sea he was still holding on to the salvation he had gotten the year before and had a heart burden to make his new-found faith known in his district. Now he was the only believer of that church in East End, and though he could only manage to read the low keys of the Bible, nevertheless he wanted to preach.

There was a little, aged man here from the U.S.A., affiliated with the Church of God, by the name of Ezra Sheets whom Dad invited to do way side preaching. Later, with the help of Captain Charles Glidden and Brother Hopkins of West Bay, a congregation was established, and soon a place of worship was built. Thus came the Church of God of East End. As a youth I became attached to that church with plans of studying for the ministry when I was finished with school. I was, from a child, always a Bible student, and even at 12 years of age could contend with any one I met in Bible truths; so by the time I reached 14 years, I saw many conflicts between popular preaching and the Bible facts, and this drove me into deeper studies of the Bible than I had ever done before.

As much as I loved my father and the Church of God, by the time I was 15 years of age we parted company, and I became a Seventh Day Adventist, a religion hated then by one's own mother. Until now I live by a very special philosophy: If the Bible says it, I believe it. If the Bible doesn't say it, then it's not for me. So in my heart that settles it. Nevertheless, there were never any hard feelings or resentments between my Dad and myself, and he still depended on me to help him plan his sermons.

Back in 1934 the island was still in the second degree stage of primitiveness. The caboose and firewood together were the source of cooking. Throughout the island, except in rare cases, kerosene lamps and lanterns gave light for homes and public gatherings as well. There were no fridges or freezers; no radios or televisions. I often question with myself in these days of electric living, "How did we survive the old days?" This comes more forcefully to mind when the current supply goes off as it sometimes does now. Back then, a major task was keeping the kitchen supplied with firewood on a day-to-day basis. I had to travel two miles or more over some rugged terrain, sometimes knee-deep in water, getting into the buttonwood, sometimes twice for the week, to cut firewood, nearly always battling swarms of mosquitoes in the process.

My mind often goes back to the old days when young people didn't have time to get in trouble. Young people, boys and girls alike, had their appointed tasks to perform at home, and knew better than to refuse doing what they were told to do. "Go and do as I say, and none of your mouth", was the first warning. The next could be a swipe with anything close at hand, reasonable to strike with. Life would be so much different for our young people today if there were only some old-time mothers and fathers around. In my youth, to avoid a flogging, I walked the straight path both with my grandfather and my Dad when he was around, and outside of my close family I also paid heed to any adult, related or not.

At that time, my Dad was absent more than he was on the Island. I used to think, "Dad has it made; he packs his sea bag and goes travelling to all those foreign lands that I may never get to see." Even as I studied geography in school, and read of such places as Europe, China, Japan and even the Americas, I used to say I would love to go to some of the places, but Cayman schooners couldn't go there, so for sure I would never see them. They all seemed so far away. Today, what major country on this planet is there that Caymanian seamen have not gone to? I know now that my father hadn't been anywhere or seen anything other than a hard life in his day as he plowed the ocean on those sailing vessels. Rather than envy him of his 'pleasure trips' I find it necessary to love and appreciate him more than ever before for those rough and trying days he endured to raise me.

Of course, life at home wasn't a continuous moonlight picnic either. In those days most children were kept busy doing one thing or another. For example, all the water we used had to be carried from the well, so every morning sufficient water for the day's need, even the laundry, had to be fetched. My aunt's time was taken up with making the thatch ropes that were traded for goods, and my grandfather was a cultivator and also raised hogs, so my little input was needed at an early age both with the ropes and the hogs. When I began to grow up, I thought if I never saw another hog it would be too soon for me. When I became a little more mature, and could go alone, there were those terrible cows to look after. Calves had to be penned in the evenings, and the cows milked in the mornings, and that usually under the invasion of thousands of mosquitoes. There was firewood to be cut and carried, and year-round there were cultivations to help take care of. If the present-day generation could be called upon to experience a year of what folks of old endured, I am sure many of them would be fixing to commit suicide before the second year. In North Side and East End just the mosquitoes alone would be sufficient to keep many hundreds of people house-bound for many days. There were those many week-long rainy days when the smoke box had to be kept fixed up inside the house all day and all night long. In those spells, wherever one went the smoke had to be taken along as a survival kit. You talked about Nehemiah in the Bible working with men on the walls of Jerusalem with their tools in one hand and a sword in the other? Well, that is a picture of the old Grand Cayman work force when it was time for the mosquitoes to invade. The Mosquito Control Unit has done a magnificent job in the past 20 years in controlling that army. Except that the mosquitoes were brought under control, tourism would never have matured in Grand Cayman.

I had no brothers or sisters to call on for help with the rugged chores of life on a daily basis. Along with attending school, performing all of the demands that came my way was really taxing on a boy. My stepmother had no limit to what she would attempt to do, and she pushed me to the same degree. Working in the cultivation in the heat of the day didn't bother her one single bit; that is until later years when sickness took over her life.

There was one aspect though that she could not participate in—the cows. There was an old black mother cow that hated the very scent of my stepmother. She dared not ever go close to that cow, especially when it had a young calf. Cows were really my biggest resentment during my youth. Sometimes it took me a week searching to find a straying cow. But we had them, and so I had to care for them. When my father came home from sea, one of the first questions to me could be, "How are the cows, son?" Dad was so attached to his cows that when the time came to butcher one he never stayed around to see it slaughtered. He knew them by names, and when he went to see them he stood by the gate and yelled for Molly or Bessie and soon they all came with their tails on their backs expecting a hand out, which he would always be carrying for them. I used to think, "It's good for you Daddy to pet up those rebels. If you had to battle them like I do you wouldn't find it such great pleasure."

Here then are just some of my boyhood experiences: attending cows, cutting firewood, keeping cultivations, as well as keeping the fish supply fresh in the home—all of these things plus six or seven hours a day, five days a week in school. Only when Daddy happened to be home to help me, then the load was not that great. As I look back on it, however, that was a conditioning process for manhood.

■

The date was 12 December 1936, I had reached 14 years of age, and that very week my beloved teacher told me, "Wilbur, I am sorry boy, but we will have to part ways now." Seating me across the teacher's table from him, he went on to say, "Under the circumstances I can't do more for you; so you won't be coming back here in January." That made me very sad because I loved to go to school more than anything else at that time, and my heart had been set on doing the Jamaica Local Third Year studies. Many of my special friends would still be in school, from whom I hated to be parted. I was already feeling cut off from my boyhood days and entering into an unknown future. However, for the next year or so, the routines of the past only dropped school days to increase more outdoor activities.

Early in 1937 my father was off on another ocean voyage, this time on the *Albert H,* a schooner that did salvaging of wrecks saving scrap iron and other metals and selling it in Panama. He returned home barely in time for Christmas. That, he used to say, was the most profitable trip he had ever made to sea. He brought home enough goodies to have opened a small store; so much that the schooner brought him to East End. Now his profession was cooking, but on that voyage he was a certified diver working with Captain Albert Bodden.

Dad said he always followed the Spirit's leading, and the Spirit told him not to go back out in January. It did seem that he was very right. By the middle of January 1938 he received a message from Jamaica to go there right away, passage paid, on the *Cimboco* which was sailing the next day to join one of the Webster's steam ships, the *Alister*, as chief cook. (James Webster, originally from Bodden Town, had migrated to Jamaica and made it big in sailboats and steamboats.) The job on the Webster line offered my father what he had never been accustomed to: a set monthly wage, with decent sleeping quarters, and lots of supplies. He used to jokingly say years after, when he joined the ship he saw things in the storeroom that he didn't know how to use. He had a great chief steward which made all the difference for him. Let me get ahead of myself to finish that part of my father's life story. The *Alister* sailed from Kingston, Jamaica to New Orleans, U.S.A., on a regular schedule. Daddy just hung on there like it was the last job he would ever have. He was away for some time, and my stepmother would go to Jamaica to meet him.

When the war started in Europe and turned into World War II, he was still Chief Cook on the *Alister*. Then finally my stepmother took sick and had to have major surgery in Kingston, so he had to take a trip off to take care of her and then take her home, intending to rejoin the ship on the next voyage to Jamaica. But this was where the Lord worked for me. Only a few days after he was home, the *Alister* was torpedoed and sunk just south of East End Lighthouse, struck by a German submarine at 4 o'clock in the morning. The relief cook for Dad went down unseen as did the Captain, Chattman Bodden from Little Cayman, Wilfred Connolly and Burns Connolly of East End, along with others. That was 29 May 1942, long to be remembered by man. There had been six survivors—Leonzie Conolly from East End, Stafford Ebanks' brother, somebody from Cayman Brac, and three from Jamaica—and Leonzie told me it had happened without warning. The ship was on its way from Texas to Jamaica, and with the route they had taken they had passed just south of Grand Cayman. The torpedo apparently hit the ship on one side and went right through the other side. She went down so fast that only the ones on deck were saved—Leonzie was on watch; that's how he survived—but they spent almost a day-and-a-half on a life raft before they were picked up by a ship headed for Puerto Rico. Ironically, my father had been working on that ship for two years, but he had gotten off before that trip because my stepmother was ill; the man who filled in for him was one of the ones who died.

Just about that time my grandfather died, and I left East End for a while to work in George Town, earning my own money even though not enough to make me rich. Cayman was still quite undeveloped as such, and there was little to do by way of earning a living. Machete work was just about the only thing for a young man unless he could get on a fishing schooner to go turtling, but, since each captain looked at his own blood first, that went to only a limited few living outside of West Bay. Anyway I fell into good company in town. Through my uncle, Barrett Welcome, I got a job with Mr. Ellery Merren, one of the loveliest man I have ever known. Three shillings per day was my pay, but Mr. Ellery had me working with him at nights in the store doing whatever there was to be done before the next day's business, and he never made me go hungry. He always gave me ready-to-eat groceries and saw to it that I received just compensation for my time. During the days I chopped bush and did odd jobs for Dr. Roy McTaggart; he always had plenty of work to be done. Sometimes Mr. Carley Merren employed me also.

Snooping on Cayman

Life in George Town of course was much harder for me than it had been at home, but then I was on my own. I wasn't by any means a wild fellow, never smoked or drank in my life, but somewhat fickle-minded as to which girl should be my real girl friend. Sure, I much understand today's young people who live in developed, fast-living world. In my day there was not the excitement we have today, but we went after what we had anyway.

Young people of today can't wait to fly away from their nest. However, there is a vast difference between home life 100 years ago and today's style of living. Home restrictions of old were similar to a military camp for the youths. I remember, being then past 20 years of age and enlisted in the Home Guard, going home on my first weekend pass, five days in all. I worked hard keeping Dad's cultivation the Thursday and Friday, and Saturday night I went up in the district and visited my current girlfriend. Well, her parents had late company, and so I had a good excuse to stay there until after 9 p.m. since on Sunday evening I would be going back to camp. I reached home near to 10 p.m. What do you think? There was Dad sitting in his rocking chair, waiting up for me.

"Now son", said he, "I love you dearly, and I know you think yourself a man now, but this is my house, and as long as you are under this roof my rules stand for you. My bed time is nine o'clock and I expect you to be inside by then." I wasn't one to argue with my father. He was the king in his own castle, and all others must obey the king's rules.

Today, I think one of the great problems with society is that parents are no longer the rulers in their homes. Unlike days of old, parents of today are being ruled and overruled by their children who do what is right in their own eyes, which for the greater part adds up to youthful foolishness. "Foolishness is bound in the heart of child," says the Bible.

In these times I thank God for my strict aunt and grandfather who controlled my early days, and then my godly father who guided me into manhood. My dear father's counsels and advice, which he gave at every opportunity, have remained with me. Dad often wrote me letters when he was away from home, and I wrote him back long, personal replies. We communicated with each other, present or absent. My Dad was the greatest person on earth to me after my grandfather Simpson Jackson and my beloved Aunt Florrie.

I hadn't really known my father in the first six years of my life—after my mother died, he had been away at sea without coming home—but then we got acquainted after he came home, and I got to love him so much. He was a tall, powerful man, 230 pounds, and such a loving and generous father. For instance, I asked him to buy me a bicycle, and he rightly said there's no place in East End to ride a bicycle, but he bought me it anyway. There I was, with the first bicycle ever to come to East End, but nowhere to ride it. I think it cost 10 pounds and that was a lot of money back then. I remember being about six years old, going to the cultivation with him, and he would put me in the basket and carry me on his back for about half-a-mile. He set such an example for me in his generosity, his morals and his values. The things that I stand for, and am known for, came from him.

3

CHANGING CAYMAN

In the Cayman Islands, the place that time forgot, life all through the '30s and into the '40s remained somewhat even as at the beginning of the century. There was hardly any money, and but little to spend it on. Clothings were limited to be had whether for men or women, except those home-sewn. The average man of those days either went to sea or used a machete and an axe as a means of living. Of course one hardly saw any enchantments to spend money on, unlike today's advertisements on televisions, radios, and the newspapers as well, that beckon everybody to lavish more and more money for "essential" items which are bought only because they look good to the eyes and are fashionable. The first suit of clothes I ever owned my father posted to me from New Orleans, for which I was so happy; but guess what? When I tried to wear my beautiful new suit there was no way I could fit into it. Boy, wasn't I sad and disappointed.

My dear grandfather died in the process of time, my Aunt Florrie was married and living a distance away, and my stepmother became very sickly in her middle age, so home life then became very rugged for me. I had no sister or near relative to help me. The war in Europe started in September 1939, and England soon became involved in battling the Germans' forward march through Europe. By 1941 things were looking bad for the British Empire, even for the unknown Cayman Islands. German submarines were operating all around the West Indies, while England was taking an unbearable pounding by German bombers. The long before spoken words of the famous Lord Nelson—"England expects every man to do his duty"—echoed in the ears of Caymanian men, and they volunteered for service from all the Islands to help in the struggle.

The call came for men to join the Trinidad Royal Navy Volunteer Reserve and the response was great; almost everyone who could pass the test tried his luck in Trinidad. Then there was the Royal Marines Merchant Navy. Caymanians were not afraid of even the merchant navy when ships were being destroyed by the German subs everywhere as so many whales had been well captived by the old time whaling ships. Caymanians gained their fame as world-renowned seamen. Many of them did not return home but they died as heroes, fighting for a just cause.

Then came the Home Guard to watch the coastline of the island, for what little good it would have done. I once sailed with a German 2nd mate with National Bulk Carriers who seemed to have known more about the coastline of Grand Cayman than even I did. He said he had been a lieutenant on a submarine stationed in the Caribbean Sea, and that they had made frequent trips ashore in Kingston, Jamaica at nights in rubber boats. They bought fresh fruits, bread, beers, or whatever, even went to the movie sometimes, and no one ever suspected them for who they were. The same for Grand Cayman—at least three times they were ashore here: once on South West Point, and twice on what is now Seven Mile Beach. On South West Point, he said one time he saw four soldiers on foot who never even looked in his direction. He went all the way to the American base just spying out their security. I know the man was telling the truth; his only opponents were more mosquitoes than he had ever seen in his life. That, of course, is only one known case of Germans among us during the war.

Anyway, Caymanian young men heeded the call to join the Home Guards and did their best whenever they were needed. They were well trained for the occasion by people such as Sergeant Hyfield who was a Canadian and unmerciful in the execution of his duties. His favourite saying on parade was, "You may break your mother's heart but you'll never break mine, you son of a, left, right, left, right." We were trained to shoot, and there were many good marksmen in the regiment.

The Home Guard was appointed to a round-the-island guard duty. Starting from Barker's in West Bay we reached all the way to Gorlin Bluff in East End and Grape Tree Point, North Side. Normally four men under a corporal manned each station. (The U.S. Navy then had a token presence in Grand Cayman, but exercised their finest duty in going after skirts and dresses.) Submarines were commonly seen around the Island. One day I was on watch atop East End lighthouse when I spotted one of them just behind the reef. We reported quickly to the Central Reporting Office (CRO) which looked after those things. They contacted the U.S. Navy and, eventually, a plane went over, but it took so long that by the time the plane appeared the sub must have been in Little Cayman.

Those were tragic years on the ocean. U-boats just seemed to be everywhere at the same time even around the Cayman Islands. The same German who told me of his exploits around the islands said he saw the *Cimboco* time and again, even followed her into anchorage at East End once after sunup one morning. They were trying to certify some silver-looking things on her deck that turned out to be aluminum drums with kerosene oil. He said they weren't about to destroy her because she was harmless; only keeping the islanders alive. So even a German's heart can be soft sometimes, in spite of war.

■

In the 1940s, starting with the war days, a visible change began to be felt and seen over the Cayman Islands financially. Families who never owned a pound note to lay aside in their lives began to boast about their bank books in the Government saving bank which was all the banking facility there was in those faraway days. That savings bank was in a little building across the street from the Post Office. It had been the location of the Competent Authorities Office that controlled anything that had to be rationed during the War. When the war came to an end, they used the same building for the Government Savings Bank and eventually that moved into the Post Office building and then into the Glass House.

Money began coming in from the men of the Trinidad Royal Navy Volunteer Reserve, as well as the merchant navy, who had allotments being paid to their families at home every month; thus Caymanian families began to live, like an old lady used to say, 'sumptuously', no longer dependent on thatch ropes as before times for a total existence. Even the Home Guard boys with their eight or ten pounds per month could contribute something toward the betterment of society. Here and there a wire-spring bed was set up. Chairs began to be seen in vacant living quarters—vacant, that is, of furnishings. The old banana-trash beds gave way to cotton mattresses. Next, thatch leaves as roofing left the scene to be replaced by zinc, and the old wooden window spaces gave way to glass windows. What a fixing up that was. Some of the real old-timers though, mind you, wouldn't agree to having glass windows in their house even when the younger members wanted to install them. My dear father could in no way be persuaded to change either windows or doors in his house. For the sake of my stepmother, I managed to persuade him to allow me to set up a nice mattress in his room. He had a spring bed by then but insisted on keeping his old banana-trash bed. Well, he complained of back aches for a little while from sleeping on a mattress but soon settled down to enjoy it. The bed was a great blessing for my stepmother; of course it was a luxury in those days. Bed frames were commonly made locally from mahogany and either floored with cow's hide, boards or else strapped with straw rope. These four-posters, as they were called, adorned many a master's bedroom, and I dare say a good price would be paid for such an antique today.

Right shortly after World War II, indeed a drastic change in society took place. Going backwards down memory's lane, we have just been reminded that many people soon changed their sleeping arrangement by burning their bed-beg-infested banana-trash bed in favour of a spring mattress to sleep on. Now we may cast our eyes in the kitchen with the rafters and some of the sides all smutty with the smoke of many years from firewood used in the old caboose. All over the Islands for past years wood had been the cooking fuel, but something more charming suddenly appeared on the horizon for which rich and poor alike flipped over; I speak of the kerosene stove. That was cleaner to work with but did not leave food with the lovely smoked flavour produced by wood fires. The stoves were more expensive to operate, but who worried? Some people hadn't been accustomed to money anyway and now had more than they had seen in their lives. Buying a stove was certainly far easier than tearing through cliffs and swamps, battling mosquitoes, to cut firewood. The first hardware store had been started by someone from Jamaica—they sold paints, kerosene stoves, radios, things like that—and kerosene, with the war over, was cheap to buy.

However, despite these developments, there were still a few old stoves to be fueled with firewood, but even in that angle things had changed; there were wood cutters who cut and sold wood by the cord island wide, and there were also those who bought and sold from trucks. During the decade of the '50s the sun even shone brighter for many families as National Bulk Carriers found employment for every able-bodied man who wanted a job; that was a bright shining star in Caymanians' crown. The next great step forward was the lighting fixtures. George Town and the surrounding areas had electricity on a token basis, but the country parts were still left with the sun, moon and stars to look to for light at nights, whether at home or in public gatherings. Then along came the Tilley lamps (made by the Coleman company and still used by campers today) that you could pump up, and they used either kerosene or white gas. The light was much brighter than any ordinary wick lamp would make.

Here and there along the way, a shining kerosene fridge found its way in homes, and lots of women laid away their old coal iron to use gas irons for ironing their clothes. Yes, the '50s and the '60s saw many changes around the Islands for better living because of post-war technologies and a little cash in the pockets of people, which was not there before. Again we take a step backward into time to have a peep into the dark chasms of yesteryear. The most essential improvement ever to reach the eastern and northern districts was when, in the middle '30s, Mr. A. W. Cardinall, the then United Kingdom Commissioner, connected those deserted, forsaken parts of Grand Cayman by road.

Much has been said concerning the difficulties and hardships that attended the path of the people of the north and the east in every angle of living because of the problems of travelling anywhere away from their homes, and there was even a saying that Grand Cayman ended at Pease Bay, Bodden Town. The roads that came into being in Cardinall's time were not after the manner of super highways, but indeed they were as heaven's blessings to those who needed help out of seclusion, although conveyances to and from the district were very limited for several years after the road went through because there were not sufficient vehicles to meet the demands island-wide. Large trucks travelled from the districts certain days of the week, on which passengers rode and were able to take produce to town to sell and then take back home whatever their purchases were. The trip was always slow and long, but they always got there.

The few vehicles around during the war sometimes were without tyres. Even gasoline was sometimes hard to obtain, to keep moving. At that time Mr. Berlon Ebanks of North Side had an old homemade bus with which he made daily runs to town, but sometimes he had to roll on solid tyres, so did Mr. Lonsdale Pouchie of East End. The buses were basically a wooden frame fixed to a car chassis. They could carry about 12-15 people, and with those solid tyres it was a rough ride. Anyway, the war being left behind, everything began picking up. From then on, cars started rolling into Grand Cayman until now there are as many cars as there are Caymanians around.

Just at war's end bananas became the big thing in the southern U.S. Many of the ex-navy Caymanian seamen got jobs on the banana boats, and though the wages counted small yet it added up in taking the precedence over doing nothing at home and surviving hard times. The fame of the Caymanian seamen was spreading around, and once he reached the right place he could always have a job.

At home, too, local opportunities sprang up when several ships came into the possession of companies such as the Kirkconnells of Cayman Brac and H. O. Merren in Grand Cayman. The *M. V. Mizpah* was the pride of the Merren's fleet; then there were the *Merco, Bodmer* and the *Antarus*. These all carried Caymanians as their crew, while the Kirkconnells owned several ships that benefited Brackers who wanted a job. There were also several independent ship owners around the islands. The lumber and banana trade was the big thing in the immediate post-war days.

4

THE JINXED SHIP

By now, I have strayed somewhat from my personal life experiences with which I started this manuscript. During the hot and fearful time of World War II, I was serving in the Home Guard at the time of the sinking of a ship just outside of George Town Harbour. That indeed was a home-learned lesson of the terrors of war; just seeing the shocking condition of those survivors. The *Cimboco* had gone out and picked them up off the life-rafts. We had no hospital, so they were put in the Town Hall. There were five of them, Norwegians. The ship had caught fire, and you didn't know whether they were white or black—they were so badly burnt all over and covered in black oil. It was pitiful. We were trying to look after them as best we could, until they could be taken to Jamaica for treatment, but I think two of them died before they got there.

Right after the war was over and the Guard was disbanded, I decided, as all my life's ambition had been, I wanted to go abroad and seek out a better life. There was a schooner by the name of *Armistice* preparing to sail to Belize and, being told that she was taking on passengers, I booked a passage, hopefully to get easily from Belize to the U.S.A. However, after spending a couple of weeks there I saw no bright prospect of getting out soon, so when the ship made her return trip to Belize I decided to head back home.

Within a week or two after reaching back home, I received a call to join the Police Force. I accepted the offer and was soon Constable Jackson. I can only say I enjoyed being a policeman for three years before I became restless with the sea itch and wanted to join the many Caymanian men who sailed the seas. I resigned my job, and even before my resignation was acknowledged, I sailed away from Grand Cayman on the *M. V. Arbutus,* a locally-owned vessel of 100 tons owned by Captain Warren Bodden. Captain Bodden had moved from Cayman to Tampa with his family, but made frequent trips to Cayman. The *Arbutus* was a fairly large hull for her times, and traded between Florida and Nicaragua. Well, I felt great just to be going to America, the land that I had by then thought of as part of Heaven on earth. I had no idea what was in store.

Our first port after leaving Cayman was Pensacola, Florida. The ship was loaded with mahogany lumber coming from Costa Rica in Central America, to be off loaded in Pensacola. Waiting there for loading was a load of general cargo, plus iron pipes for Puerto Cabeza, Nicaragua, destined for the gold mine. The second day out of Pensacola, the nor'wester of the year came down on us. What a storm! There was no way to shut down the bilge pump and stay afloat. Mr. Delores Whittaker stayed at the wheel for more than 12 hours, and then the Captain relieved him for several hours before the weather began to lull; by then the deck load of pipes had gone in the deep. We stumbled into Cape San Antonio with four feet of water in the cargo hold; even the engine-room floor was awash. We spent three days there drying out and then proceeded on to Nicaragua. After unloading what remained of the cargo we sailed on down the coast to Puerto Lemon, Costa Rica, taking on another load of mahogany. From there on the *Arbutus* became my home for more than a year as we went all over the Western Hemisphere, including the Pacific Sometimes we had general cargo and sometimes dynamite for various countries, but always it was lumber back to the U.S.A.

After the first year, I left the ship in Cayman Brac for a vacation. In those days getting to Grand Cayman from Cayman Brac was like getting to America from Cayman. I waited in the Brac for three weeks to get transportation out, by which time I married a pretty 16-year-old girl, Trilby Jackson. I was 22 years old. That marriage, of course, didn't work much in my favour, although I struggled hard to keep it going for 15 years. Only a week after reaching home from the Brac I left on the *Merco* to go to Tampa, Florida to join the *Mizpah.* She was hauling bananas from Puerto Mexico into Brownsville, Texas, sometimes Mobile. The *Mizpah* was a clean, fast and comfortable little ship, but after six months seeing the same faces and places I became restless and wanted to move on to greener pastures. That urge and decision almost cost me my life.

Coming into Mobile, at the end of one voyage, we happened to be docked just astern of a sleek-looking ship that took the appearance of a United Fruit Company ship, which I thought she was. I soon learned that she had been bought by two Norwegians, Captain Bakken and Chief Engineer Gerrard. I decided I wanted a job on that ship. In only a short while I gained an interview with the Captain and was hired on the spot as the Chief Cook for the *M.V. Thalia*. Captain Theo refused to sign me off from the *Mizpah*, but the immigration signed me on to the *Thalia's* articles because she was sailing that day from Mobile while the *Mizpah* was there indefinitely between charters.

From here on for the next six months the *Thalia's* log book makes a large history book. The happenings and occurrences on board that ship just might seem unreal to the readers. Leaving Mobile Saturday evening, we were bound for the port of Miami where on Monday they would start loading refrigerated cargo for Puerto La Cruz, Venezuela and heavy equipment for Maracaibo. However, it wasn't until Wednesday that she arrived in Miami, under tow, with a broken shaft. In just a couple of days in the dry dock she was declared ready for sea. Quickly the waiting cargo was being loaded on. Thousands of eggs went into the aft cargo hold. There were tons of frozen meats and chicken for No. 2 hold. Then there were fruits, beers, and, you name it—we had it onboard. Last of all was a deck load of Lincoln Continental cars and a tractor or two.

We pulled away from Pier 3 in Miami around 10 p.m. one night and started down the channel toward the open sea, bound for Venezuela. I had only just stretched out in my bunk to relax when, without notice, I was on my cabin floor. Trying to pick myself up from the floor I found it was not possible to stand to one's height unless hanging onto something. Right away I knew the ship was grounded hard and fast. No efforts could free her off the bar that night. The morning came and the Coast Guard tugs got to work, but at the most could only straighten her from her 40-degree list. A large barge and crane went to work unloading the heavy deck load to lighten her up lest damage should be done to the bottom. With that she was floated and taken back to Pier 3 for divers' inspection.

The divers decided the damage done was not sufficient to merit going into dry dock, so in another couple of day we were on our way again. We reached Puerto La Cruz in record time without incidents, where some of the cargo was off-loaded. Then it was on to Maracaibo for the rest of the unloading. Our emergency order was to go down quickly to Santa Martha, Colombia to load on bananas that were overdue for shipment because the ship that was to load them had broken down in mid-ocean. At a high speed, we got rid of the cargo and left Maracaibo Lake at mid-day on a Saturday, but, and there was a big "but", the Captain sailed away without a pilot on board. So, you guessed it! When we reached the pilot station, the Coast Guard boarded us. The order was to anchor the ship in a specified place, and the Captain and Chief Engineer were taken in custody. Four guards remained on board, and it was not until Monday afternoon that the Captain and Chief were brought back onboard. The fine had been US$10,000 for sailing without a pilot.

We finally reached Santa Martha and received the bananas, but in poor shape, and although we reached Miami in no time at all—the *Thalia* was a very fast ship, cruising at 18 knots—the greater part of those bananas was taken out of the cargo hold with a steam shovel to be dumped. However, that was not the ship's fault; it was already a perished cargo before being put onboard.

The next problem was that there was no money with which to pay the crew. Nevertheless, everyone thought, now everything will be normal onboard the *Thalia* and with the crew from here on. The crew consisted of a part United Nations of 21 men. To be sure this was not a company of hoodlums, but more trouble lay ahead of us.

■

At this point, the *Thalia* had to be taken out to sea from Miami to clean the cargo holds of the rotten bananas, and with that done she returned to Pier 1 where loading began of perishables and frozens to be taken to Laguira, Venezuela. Once again, even as the previous voyage, the holds were packed with eggs, meats and chicken, apples, pears and grapes. The deck load was even more awesome this time. There were Cadillacs most beautiful, brand-new; tractors and supply tanks; even two small planes were squeezed in on the boat deck. The stevedores had worked almost through Friday night to complete loading, preparing for sailing on Saturday, however, when we should have been leaving Miami, first there was a power blackout to take care of, then it was discovered that the cargo refrigeration wasn't working as it should. Even though electricians worked late into the night from ashore, by Sunday morning the *Thalia* was yet not ready for sea. Not until Monday would it be possible to get some needed generator parts down from Jacksonville.

Sunday was a very quiet day on the Miami waterfront. In the afternoon, an old colored man, along with what might have been two of his grandsons, could be seen on the end of the pier with his rod and reel casting for either his Sunday supper or Monday lunch.

I had just a few days before become the Chief Steward on board and was showing my skills in having a real mouth-watering supper prepared. My Bahamian Chief Cook wasn't very efficient so I had to stay around the kitchen. The *Thalia's* kitchen was situated on the port side just aft of midship and open to the main deck, so from the kitchen one could look right across the dock and see the happenings. Well we were just in the process of serving supper at 5 p.m., the usual time, when the old colored fisherman who had been fishing on the end of the pier shouted in the kitchen window, "There's fire out here, fire, fire!"

I jumped out quickly to see what was happening. I ran back to the wheel-house and rang the fire alarm. By then billows of smoke ascended from No. 3 hatch even though it was sealed and a Cadillac was parked on top of it. So there we were; now a burning ship! Anyway Miami City has what it takes to master fires, and in no time at all a part of the fire brigade was assembled on Pier 1.

The Cadillac had to first be lifted off, and luckily the heat hadn't been severe enough as yet to cause it to blow. More than 1,000 wooden crates of eggs had to be unloaded to the dock to reach the cause of the fire. It was late in the night before the firemen were satisfied that the fire was completely extinguished. Never did I see so many roasted eggs in one place. Every crate had to be taken out to be sure there was nothing more burning. The fire must have burned from the night before, but lacked sufficient oxygen to push it into a flame. All day Monday and into the night the refrigeration experts worked to renew the system and make it as safe as possible.

By Wednesday afternoon No 3 was reloaded, everything of machinery for ship's operation was checked and declared in running order, and that evening, once again, the *Thalia* headed out to sea. The Chief Engineer and two sensible crew members left in Miami.

The ship was dangerously overloaded for a voyage down to Cuba, let alone to Venezuela, and there were lots of doubts concerning a safe trip across. The weather was beautiful as we sailed by the north-east coast of Cuba and into the south coast of Haiti. This was just what the *Thalia* needed, and it just seemed perfect cruising for 19 men of 10 different nationalities united as a team to man a ship on the ocean, only they all seemed to have forgotten the ship they were controlling was the *M. V. Thalia*, concerning which the word "jinxed" had often been used recently. I was beginning to wonder why I was staying on this ship. Was it worth so much just being called Chief Steward? Anyway, I thought to myself, when I reach back in Miami I'll be going to New York.

That night, as we left the coast of Haiti behind us and headed towards Venezuela, the calm and beautiful ocean we had enjoyed since leaving Miami began to boil up into foam. By the next morning we were in a raging tempest. The wind was gale force. By breakfast time the ship was pitching and tossing so wildly we decided to skip trying to fry eggs and bacon. All that day and through the night the storm pounded the ship; barely could she be kept in steerage way, but that was our only hope of weathering the storm—by standing head on to the waves. By 9:30 the next morning a squall out of the east came over with greater fury than any before. The situation was dangerous indeed, but Captan Bakken was an old North Sea Master accustomed to fighting gales of such dimensions. He fought the weather with the *Thalia* like one battling a ferocious lion in an arena. This was our fifth day out of Miami, and we should have been in Laguira by now, but here we were only hoping to make it some other day. Then it all happened ... so suddenly it could hardly be seen happening ... the ship had gone down on her port side, hopelessly over.

She had gotten cross way in the tempest and the billows were dashing over her like on a reef. The engine-room staff managed to reach the deck, saying the engines were flooded, and just then everything went deadly quiet below. Here was a dead ship just waiting to be buried in the depths, but we didn't have long to wait for the ceremony to be performed.

Can I ever forget those crucial moments with the *Thalia* listed over on her side with half of her deck submerged?

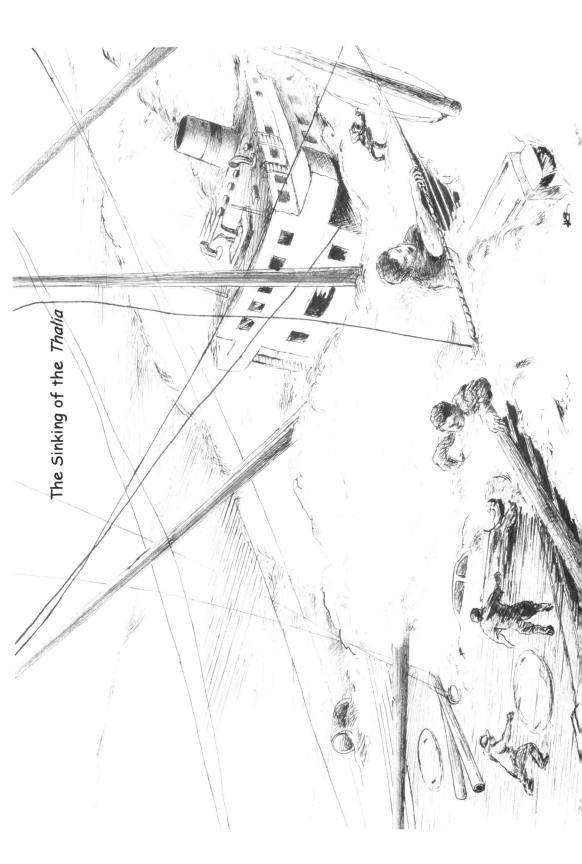

The Sinking of the *Thalia*

There was no way of even cherishing the thought of a lifeboat to save us. The port boat had already been crushed to pulp by a large truck that was stowed between the two boats and had slipped its lashings and gone in the deep. A 28-wheeler supply truck that hung over the stern had also parted company with us and gone floating away. The ship was in grave difficulty, and I closed my eyes and prayed to the Lord to take us in His care.

When I had finished praying I opened my eyes to see the horizon for the help I believed my God would send. We were all huddled there in one spot, hanging on for dear life. We had good life belts, but what could they do for us in such a tempest, and so far from anywhere? Visibility was short because of the pouring, constant rain, but I saw just what I expected to see—a large beautiful ship coming right at us. No one else had seen that ship. They all thought I was having hallucinations when I said there is a ship out there. Can you imagine the hopes and joys that automatically sprang up in the hearts of 19 seemingly lost souls stranded on the side of a sinking ship? There were only a couple of passing minutes after sighting our rescuers that the *Thalia* straightened herself on an even keel and took a quick plunge into the depths headfirst.

The rescue ship was still some way off when the *Thalia* took her plunge, but we all had a reprieve temporarily when the wooden top of the crew's quarters aft on the ship floated off in one whole piece when she was going down. All of us could climb onto that and hang on, at least safe from the sharks at the moment. The ship, a large tanker by the name of *Samuel C. Loveland*, of Italian registry and crew, first tried to launch a lifeboat to rescue us but failed to do so in such a tempest. A cargo boom was then swung out with a steel basket attached to the cable that could lift about five people at a time out of the water. The ship, of course, was held head into the weather to minimise the rolling and tossing. Each man had to swim 100 yards or more from our perch to get over the sunken basket and stand into it. Three damaged men had to be helped first into the basket, but in the process of time every one was saved from their watery grave. Early the next morning we were in Puerto La Cruz, Venezuela, survivors of a jinxed ship, but my ordeal, at least, was not yet over.

5

SUCCESS
AT SEA

Early in the morning after we had been picked up, the tanker *Samuel C. Loveland* entered Puerto La Cruz where a hassle began between the ship's agent and immigration concerning the fate of the 19 surviving seamen. The ill ones, three in number, were admitted to a hospital, no problem, but all that day no word about the status of the other 16 until late that evening, as the ship was preparing to sail, that the Creole Oil Corporation of Venezuela had finally taken on the responsibility for all of us from government. The next day, the two distressed British subjects—Tommy Douglas and myself—at the request of the British Ambassador, were put on a bus for Maracaibo. There we stayed for day after day, week after week, for three long months. Never could he get any recognition from Grand Cayman concerning either of us. Mr. Herbert, the Ambassador was indeed a kind gentleman. He took proper care of us because we were in the DBS category—Distressed British Seaman—and while I have always been a loyal subject of the Crown, that experience served to strengthen my allegiance to Great Britain.

In those three months, message after message, even our pictures, were sent to Cayman from the Ambassador's office but no word was ever returned to acknowledge us. Then finally, the Ambassador decided, whover we were, or wherever we were born, he would issue British passports to us. Now, before proceeding further with the woes that this experience dished out to us, let me speak of the great blessing we received from it. The Ambassador had told Tommy and I that the Captain of the *Thalia* informed him that he would be taking us to the U.S. soon to give us jobs on another ship he was taking over. Tickets were to be sent to us to travel to Miami, but fortunately those tickets never reached us. I say "fortunately", because the *Queen Annie II*, the ship that we should have been joining in Jacksonville, Florida sailed without us but never up to now has she ever been seen or heard of again, nor any one from her. The cook who took my place, Mr. Mattison Coe, of Grand Cayman, is termed only as "missing at sea". *Queen Annie II* was loaded with TNT bound for Belize, and that ends her story.

In Maracaibo we walked up and down every day from the hotel to the waterfront, boarding many ships just hoping for a job on one of the many English ships that came in there. We had no luck in getting shipped, but we never could be hungry. On board the ships we were given food and drinks in abundance, also we received items of clothing and shoes; even a suitcase was given to me. Each Friday the Ambassador gave us some type of clothing and some spending money. Oh, we were well cared for all those weeks in Maracaibo. Wherever we went we were treated kindly. Every one just seemed to know that we were distressed seamen from an unknown country. But without identifications there were no jobs for us. Anyway in process of time Tommy received a letter from a captain with whom he had been sailing, which came through the Ambassador's office. On a certain date Tommy was to be in Laguira to join a ship on which he had previously sailed. Well, through the Ambassador, surely Mr. Jackson will get a break there as well as Mr. Douglas. It was at that time that we were fitted with passports. We were given plane tickets to Laguira and bade the Ambassador and his lovely staff good bye.

Now we were on our own and going by faith. At the airport in Laguira we found a taxi driver who spoke English, and was much in sympathy with our plight. So, hearing that we didn't have money to pay a hotel, he took us right downtown to an old man's rundown house who took in down and out people just like us. We were happy with the setting because our cash supply was limited. So far we had been much blessed with such a kind and caring taxi driver, and here was a pleasant old man. Quickly we started on our way to the waterfront, all excited to know if the ship we were expecting was there. We were close enough to walk from the old man's house to the dock in a few minutes.

"There she is", said Tommy, all excited. "That's her anchored over there." We rented a little canoe from a fisherman at the fishing dock to go out to the ship. We paddled that canoe like two Indians late in reaching their settlement. Well, everybody just treated Tommy as a long-lost buddy, newly-found. As for me, well I was a stranger whom no one knew or cared about. The cook quickly fixed a plate of lunch—the time was just past lunch time—so Tommy was given a plate which he was about to share with me, but I refused to have any of it, so Tommy just pushed it aside on the pretext that we weren't hungry, and certainly we weren't; we had enough cans and biscuits we brought down from Maracaibo to last us several days. The main big thing for me was to know if, and how, I was getting out of Laguira, Venezuela. The captain, we were told, was asleep, but soon he came down on the deck to join the party. Warmly he shook hands with Tommy, and nodded his head to me, plainly saying in his mind, who are you, and what are you doing here? Tommy told the captain of me, giving him a run down of our sad story. He listened with but little interest. Soon he began to express regrets of our misfortunes, but my heart sank when he said he was very sorry but there wouldn't be any way he could help me. Have I ever in my life reached such a low ebb? I am sure not. Tommy tried to make a plea for help, but the Captain remained adamant; no way could he help me.

We got into our rented canoe and made our way ashore. My mind was devastated and moving in all directions. Tommy tried to assure me that he was not going to ever leave me there. I told Tommy he should go, that I would be all right, but the truth is I had become very distressed. In fact, I had already made up my mind what I would do—that night, when no one was around, I would just walk down to the waterfront and slip quietly out of sight in the murky water of the bay. I had been driven to a point of desperation—in a strange country, no money, no friends, three months of waiting, no relief in sight. Also I didn't have any money to go back to the British Ambassador in Maracaibo—as far as he was concerned we were gone from the country—and the only person I knew, Tommy, was heading off tomorrow. I didn't say anything to Tom. But I was serious about ending it all; I've never been more serious about anything in my life. That I saw as an easy and final solution in ending my woes. Since that time I never think it strange when I hear that someone committed suicide. More than once I experienced situations where I really saw death as a blessed relief from the present environment. I think St. Paul said at one point he wasn't sure which was better—life or death.

That's where I stood in Venezuela. I was in deep despair.

Returning the canoe to its owner we started walking along the dock. There were about three ships there, but our eyes caught a very strange-looking one on the far end of the dock. She flew the English flag over her stern, and we decided to go out there and check her out. What a surprise! Coming abreast of the ship we saw a couple of men leaning on the rail and looking at us. They both shouted out just about the same time, "Hey Tommy! Hello Will! Where did you all come from? You are both supposed to be drowned." These were two Cayman Brackers that both of us knew very well, and who knew us. Not more than five minutes could have passed before the entire crew was out there; each one had questions of his own concerning us. This was like we were something new just dropped down before them out of space. That indeed was just about where we came from, being first plucked out of the deep, and then lost to society; now we seemed to be getting back into civilization. Down came the Captain and Chief Mate. What a reception Tommy and I received there! The ship was the *M. V. Precise* out of Jamaica, and owned by Mr. Ashton Reid, originally of Little Cayman. The Captain was Mr. Will Ritch and the Chief Mate Mr. Sedley Ritch, both of the Brac. The crew consisted mostly of Cayman Brackers. So right away Tommy and I began to feel at home. We told them our entire life's story of the past six months and the *Thalia*, up to the moment. Tommy told them of the treatment I had received that day—the other captain refusing to help me get out of Venezuela—and that he had decided that he was staying right there with me. "Hell, no!" said Captain Ritch. "You boys will go from here on the *Precise* if I have to carry you in the crow's nest." That indeed was the most cheering news I had heard in three months. However, since Tommy wanted to get back to Miami he decided he would go with the other ship, and I would go with the *Precise*. So it was, the next morning Captain Ritch took me to the Custom's office and signed me on the articles of the *M. V. Precise* as an apprentice oiler for 10 pounds per month.

For three full years I remained on the ship and reached the highest place of trust and favour with Captain Reid. In just a couple of months I became Chief Steward there, and so became greatly trusted with the stores and feeding of the ship. Life was not always pleasant and sunny on board the *Precise*—disaster beset us from time to time—but through it all my Great Protector stood by me. Twice we went on the reef, and once we were on fire on the ocean. Once, loaded with asphalt, she sprang a leak going into Jamaica from Trinidad. We weathered a storm once that swept the deck of the entire deck load of lumber. I can only say I remained with the *Precise* those years out of appreciation for the ship that took me out of my agony in Venezuela and saved my life from being a suicide.

■

For nearly five years now I had been absent from home, so I decided to return to see my dear old father. I had never forgotten him throughout those years, writing to him regularly and always sending him some money. As well, my wife and I had parted ways, but there was a little boy to maintain. Earning in those days were small, but five pounds could purchase on an equality with today's 50 dollars. The Cayman Islands were still in semi-hibernation, emerging from a state of nothingness, gaining just a little public recognition. That was in the decade of the 1950's as Cayman seamen were becoming famous as a people of the sea. Many banana boats around the southern U.S.A. were crewed and some even mastered by Caymanians. A great many men had gotten jobs on American ships and were making good. However, a number of the men soon moved their families to wherever their home port happened to be, which meant they were not supporting the economy of the islands. Caymanians could be found from California back to Maine in the U.S.A., and Brooklyn, New York soon became a mini-Caymanian settlement. The exodus could be likened to the Jews returning to Jerusalem; we just thought of America as an earthly heaven in those days.

Back home, however, there was springing up a bright ray of hope for better things to come. The tourist industry, by the mid-50s, had begun to put forth a few little blossoms—a sign of one day producing some fruits. The Beach Club and the Galleon Beach hotels were drawing into the island of Grand Cayman a few chosen visitors, and many of those visitors of that era were buying property on the island because land was cheap at that time and a lot of it was available. Beach property, so valued by the foreigners, was "useless" as far as the natives were concerned, and many were the Caymanians who thought these foreigners were a bit crazy.

Then in 1952 a little airport was built, with help from Jamaica and the U.K., and went into operation in Grand Cayman. One man by the name of Captain Owen Roberts pioneered the plane service to the Island with a little seaplane, making the rounds once or twice per week—Kingston, Cayman, Tampa, Florida, back to Cayman and Kingston. But soon the dear man lost his life when his plane crashed in Jamaica making one such flight. But with the little airport coming into operation, the Costa Rican Airline, LACSA, began making regular weekly flights to and from Miami, and BWIA began making frequent flights in and out. As a result of those weekly flights between the two carriers, more and more foreigners got to hear about the Cayman Islands.

But there was still no air communication between Grand Cayman and the Sister Islands; only the sea linked them. By 1955, however, something big was happening in the Islands. One of the world's largest-to-be shipping companies, National Bulk Carriers, had discovered Caymanain seamen and was hiring every able-bodied man who wanted to go to sea in the company's employment. Soon, National Bulk of New York opened a shipping office in George Town with Mr. Bertie Panton as a shipping agent, and before long his office, in a little house on the site where the Bank of Nova Scotia is today, became the busiest place on the Island. Hundreds of men were regularly going and coming, and preparing to go again. Soon LACSA was making daily flights to Miami to keep the men moving.

I returned home from my extended trip in 1954, May month, and although I could have shipped out in a few days, I chose to spend six weeks at home helping my Dad with his pastures and cultivations before leaving again. During that time at home my uncle who lived in New York sent me a letter from Captain Del Bodden to come up there for a Chief Steward's job he was holding for me. Once again it just happened to be the *Arbutus* I would leave Cayman on. This time I was going straight to Jacksonville, Florida where I would sign off and go on to New York.

Everything went right well for me. I arrived in New York Sunday night by bus, and Monday evening I was on board a ship and sailing away from there. The ship was a Greek Panamanian freighter by the name of *Estero*. She had on a load of general cargo for Port au Prince, Haiti and four ports in Cuba. That was my first real job as far as wages went. Four hundred dollars per month as steward and chief cook did sound like a lot of money when compared to my top previous wage of twenty-five pounds. Of course, on the *Thalia* I was supposed to be paid US$300, but every time we hit port the captain would say "no money". Now here I was, being properly paid and on the largest bottom I had ever sailed before. She was a freighter but had accommodation for six passengers. I felt great on that job. The voyage lasted a little over one month, and we arrived back in New York with a load of salt from Inagua, Bahamas. There was some bad news awaiting us in New York: the ship was sold to Brazil. The question was, who wanted to make the trip out there to make the delivery? Not me; no way! I paid off and went ashore.

I wasn't about to lose contact with New York, that's where I always wanted to be. Captain Bodden, my uncle Rennie, my father's brother, had told me had a job, and said he would send me out again in just about a week's time. Anyway, having met a couple of Cayman Brac boys in Brooklyn the next day after I left the ship, they coaxed me into going with them to National Bulk Carriers' office in Manhattan. It was a decision that became a major turning point in my life. As I walked into the office the gentleman I saw was one I knew perfectly well from being in Jamaica. Mr. Cyril Ritch made much of me and greeted me cheerily in the presence of an office filled with people looking jobs. I felt great that day. "Jackson, you are just the man I need today," he said. "Come now. Run down to the doctor's office before noon time and get a physical for me, and come right back here." Mr. Ritch didn't ask me if I wanted a job with the company; he just gave the orders while I listened. "I want you to go down to Marcus Hook tomorrow morning on board the *Bulk Trader*; I know I can depend on you for a good job there." The ship was without a chief steward, because the Captain had fired three in just six months. Well, I didn't feel so happy with such news, but at least I was joining the great National Bulk Carriers Company. No way could I let Mr. Ritch be disappointed in me. My performance would have to be only the best in the fleet. This resolution I lived up to for 16 years with the company, and during that time I gained the reputation of being the best chief steward with the company. My last five years with National Bulk were spent relieving stewards and cleaning up their mess; at the same time training cooks and stewards. In 16 years I sailed on 28 different ships, made three complete trips around the world, and saw the five continents—quite a leap for this boy from East End.

In truth, life during those years was good for me. I did the thing that I loved best to do—helping people to enjoy food because it was nicely prepared. Seamen can be a very miserable crowd at times, or most times, and 99 times out of 100 their gripes start with the subject of food. I saw myself as a success with those I had to feed by keeping them happy, but on the personal side I was not too happy with my own life. My wife and I were divorced. My darling little daughter, the pride of my life, had died when only two years of age. I had no sisters or brothers, and of my mother I had no remembrance. So I thought at least I ought to have one woman to call my own, but not while I still had to sail the seas for a living.

Also, by then it was the mid-60s and great and rapid changes were taking place at home. Tourism was moving ahead, with hotels and guest houses springing up around the Island of Grand Cayman. Lots of ex-seamen were getting jobs ashore especially in the construction business. With the husbands away so much, family relationships in many instances were under strain. Marital relationships were turning into squabbles, and divorces were becoming very prevalent. After all, the average seaman shipping out usually found a bed to sleep in at every port. Except for the middle-aged family man, life was one string of enjoyment out there. But the dear woman of the house was held as a good piece of furniture kept in reserve for future use, so when she made a mistake, and gave in to the temptations of the flesh, divorce was usually the answer. It can however be truly said that the average Caymanian wife and mother could only be classed among the world's most faithful and discreet women. She stayed at home and attended to the business of raising her children. So often it can be said of so many, she has done exceedingly well.

6

OLD VALUES

Planning for my future was something I had lots of time for during my time at sea with National Bulk. My first marriage having ended in a divorce court, I never wanted to make the same mistake again, so I was being very cautious thinking of home and of the woman I might ask to share the remainder of my life with me. In those days East End was known only as the fishing village, and the boys coming from there to work in town were called "East End fish babies". Well, in fact there was nothing out there to charm any one more than love itself. Personally, I had always suffered with somewhat of an inferiority complex. I lived as a selfish recluse with only a minimum of social association. That, however, was not related to me alone in those lean and mean days. Prior to the mid-40s, the young men of the countryside had to go to town and do machete work in cow pastures or around peoples' yards to earn a sustenance, and many of us had to live in town under the meanest of conditions. Nevertheless, we boys could hold our heads high and see the world squarely in its face for none of us went to prison for stealing anything from anybody or for dealing in dope, or being drunk and disorderly.

Years before, during my Home Guard and police days, my eyes had fallen and my heart flipped on and for a lovely brown-skinned girl named Sybil Harris in George Town. Had I loved that girl! We had met a few times, although we never communicated—she was from one of the upper class families, and who was I? Every time I saw that girl I just wanted to at least take her hands in mine and kiss them. It would have been enough just to talk with her sometimes. Anyway, the old folks always said, "Time longer than rope." So when I got out there and saw the world, and built myself a fame, as a top chief steward, and as one who maintained an unblemished character, my mind returned to my dream girl.

Just about that that time, a respectable gentleman from George Town joined our ship for a trip or two to learn the chief steward's job, to take over another ship. He was older than I but a fine man, and we became close friends spending a great deal of time together. In the midst of a conversation one night, by chance somehow, the name of my Princess Charming was called.

Did my heart go skipping, or did it just race too fast to be mentioned? Here's where I could be my own private detective and ask some simple apparently unconcerned questions of my friend. He told me she was in his home as one of his own daughters. His daughters, of course, I knew were seen as local princesses in their community. They had recently been bereaved of their mother, and he, of a great wife. Not only was there a friendly association in a time of distress, but he let me know that my princess was related to him—a blood relative.

My next questions drew a smiling suspicion from my friend: is she married or engaged to be married? "Not really," he said. "She has a lot of admirers, but no one that she is serious about." Tell me, very seriously, I asked, do you think that lady will marry me if I ask her to? "A man like you is who she is waiting to find to be married to," was the reply. "She is a great girl and deserves the best in a husband, as I am sure you will be." With that note we ended our conversation, while my mind became cemented in the decision—I will ask Miss Sybil Harris to marry me. My ship was in the Mediterranean Sea heading into Port Said, Egypt the next day, and although it was past 10 o'clock in the night, I sat down to my desk to write a letter—the most important letter I would ever write. No, that one wasn't the right wording at all; that one went into the waste paper basket. By mid-afternoon the ship was due to arrive in Port Said, Egypt, and the agent would take all mail ashore for posting. As soon as breakfast time was over, and I had made my morning rounds to certify that my boys had all done their duties, I sat down at my desk, having talked a little with my spiritual advisor in the matter, and rewrote that letter. I closed with a direct question: "The big question is, Miss Harris, will you marry me?" That afternoon my petition was on its way, and I began watching the calendar as I waited for her reply.

We were on our way through the Suez Canal and down to Rastanura, then it would be all the way around Cape Good Hope, South Africa, and back to the U.S.A. My letter was hardly ever out of my thoughts. What would she say? Would she in fact bother to answer me at all? The weather held beautifully as day by day the ocean miles slid behind us getting us closer to port. Finally the last night of the voyage reached us, and early the next morning the port steward was onboard with lots of mail for the officers and crew. While the mail call was going on I just acted unconcerned. I knew there would be a letter from my Dad, which usually made up my count of mail, but today, my! I am getting nervous now! When my name was called, sure enough, there was a letter from Sybil Harris. What did she have to say? No, she didn't say she loved me, or yes, I'll marry you, but she did say please write me back. That to me was encouragement enough. And so began a warm mail courtship between us.

We were only in the U.S. a couple of days when the ship was on her way again. This time the charter would be from the Persian Gulf to Japan. Mail would only be had in Japan. Nevertheless, in spite of the vast distance that separated us, my girl and I through our long letters soon had built up a flaming love relationship, and before long we were making plans to get married. One day in Japan we received the good news that the ship was sailing to Kuwait to load for Rotterdam, Holland, which meant that those whose vacation was due could be relieved in Holland. I lost no time in placing my application for a relief. Our plans were then set in motion to be married in Jamaica on my way home from Holland. Sybil's baby sister was then living in Jamaica, so there was no problem in arranging a wedding there. On 30 January 1965, Miss Sybil Harris and I were married in Kingston, Jamaica by Mr. Jim Russell, a popular marriage officer. It was the best day of my life. Love and happiness have never failed us for over 31 beautiful years.

■

Looking backward into the past and seeing the present is somewhat like a man who, from early life, spends all of his days locked away somewhere without recognition of his surroundings, until one morning a door swings open and he is told to enter a world of enlightenment and knowledge. He has never driven in a motor car before. He has never known about electric lights, nor has he ever eaten ice-cream in all his life. The Cayman Islands was that sort of a wilderness dwelling. Since the earliest habitation, the settlers lived in obscurity and with privations. They had nothing, or only a little, but they worried about nothing. The fact is, the ancients knew of nothing to miss having—they had what they knew and knew what they had. The people sat down to their afternoon meal of fish and ground provisions and enjoyed it better, no doubt, than did the big man at his elaborate table with his thick slices of prime roast beef and his asparagus in white wine sauce, and all the other luxuries.

In the old Cayman, people lived a carefree, contented life. The man of the house had the Scripture fulfilled in him which says, "The sleep of a labouring man is sweet, whether he eats little or much." No one worried about how soon the bank would foreclose on their home or other possessions because they couldn't pay a loan. There was no bank in the Cayman Islands to tempt any one to reach for that which he couldn't manage. No, we didn't have much, of a truth, but that which we had was already ours. By today's standard the house was shabby and humble, but Joe's house was his own palace. His bed was made of banana trash, and his furniture only wooden, roughly-made benches, but he could enjoy every splinter of it because he owned it outright. In those days, there were no cars in the country parts, and a very few anywhere in the Islands. The horse and donkey left no overhead expenses after making a trip—they ate grass and drank water from one common watering hole. There was no gas bill, no insurance or repair costs.

By today's standard of living, my boyhood days were cash-less ones as such. Young people, like myself, started saving pennies and half pennies from January for the long wait to Christmas, and, by the way, Christmases of those days seemed like two of our present years apart. The child who had 15 to 20 shillings to spend on the 24th night of December could feel rich and happy. In the same light, the husband and father of the home, if he was a landlubber, tried to lay up in store his shillings and half crowns, and even here and there a note or two whenever possible, to meet the family's year end needs. Looking at Cayman today one might find it hard to believe that even until the middle of the 20th century there was nothing special to crow about in these Islands.

Of course, we did have an abundance of luxuries that cannot be bought on the common market today: friendliness, a genuine heart-caring concern, love for humanity, and a spirit of helpfulness for one another. For all these items the blueprints seem to have been lost, and therefore they are no longer in production.

During my youthful days in the Cayman Islands, one knew everybody and everybody knew one. As a rule it was mandatory to respect older folks. They were addressed primarily as "Uncle" this or "Aunt" that, if not "Mr." and "Mrs." Behavior was compulsory in their presence. Just any one of those old folks had the authority to lay hold to a child and whip him if necessary.

One Sunday afternoon, sitting behind an old deacon in church, my friend stuck a straight pin in the hardened part of his big toe and struck the old man in the bottom where his dungaree pant was the tightest on him. I laughed, although I had nothing to do with the actual crime. Well, you know what? The old deacon led us both out the door, and gave us a real strapping with his cow hide belt. We didn't even think of running. He then took us back inside and sat us down, one on either side of him, just like the two thieves hanging one on each side of Jesus. Did I dare go home and tell my grandfather that Uncle Fred beat me? I knew much better than that. But Monday morning, before Grandpa finished eating and drinking his bread and coffee, up came Uncle Fred—they were brothers, you see. He commenced his statement with, "That boy of yours was rude in church yesterday." He continued to state his case against me, so that I just knew I had to undergo another lashing. But then, just when my grandfather reached up to pull down his "doctor-do-good", the prosecutor pleaded mercy. "Don't beat him again. I took care of him already." Those were the children-training conditions that existed in my boyhood days, which served only to create good men and women. You can just bet whatever you treasure most that I was from then on always circumspect in Uncle Fred's presence, or anywhere else in public.

What is the difference between my experience then and the present conditions? Well in the first place Uncle Fred would have become subjected to a knuckling match with the child's father, or else a court appearance. In the old days they sternly made men out of boys, by infecting self respect, and respect for others. Children were early taught to say "good morning" or "good evening" to seniors when their paths crossed, or they met. A little boy of eight or nine recently came into my store and started addressing me as 'Will" repeating it over and over in the course of being served. I said, "Son didn't your parents tell you to say 'Mr.' or 'Mrs.' to senior people?" He replied "No. Mama tell me I don't have to bow down to nobody." I asked, "Who are you parents?" "Man and woman," was the reply. I said, "Of that I am very doubtful, boy."

We talk about moral decline and culture disappearance, but is it not that children are lacking the degree of home training that is needed to keep them in line with respectable community? Modern living and fast developments in the land should not be allowed to diminish the good morals and principles of the lovely old Cayman. What else do we have worth saving of the past?

"You may think yourself a man. but in my house bedtime is 9 o'clock."

7

A WAY OF LIFE

By now the boys and girls of my childhood have either grown old, or have passed away. The wise elders of my youth have all gone away, too, and there remains but little of yesterday to be seen today. No longer do we see even a ghost of the old Cayman anywhere in the shadows. Progress and development have totally obliterated the face of old lady Cayman. Over the entire Island of Grand Cayman and her sisters so many changes have taken place that there is no semblance of what used to be.

Sure enough, everybody wants to live in a nice house and drive in a new car, yet too many people are making themselves sick physically, or mentally, or perhaps both at the same time, by over-reaching beyond their financial abilities to keep in step with the person living on the other side of the road. As a result, so often, stress and worries dominate otherwise sound minds. In the old days, the majority, if not all families, owned their homes with no obligations to any financial institutions thus avoiding the problem of monthly mortgage payments. They didn't have much, but what they owned today was theirs tomorrow; theirs to pass on to family.

Throughout the Cayman Islands wattle-and-daub houses graced the landscape, and of these the dwellers were all downright proud to claim ownership. Join me for a minute as we look inside and outside of an old-time home. To begin with, the house is set a good distance away from the public path, leaving a spacious front yard. In the backyard is probably a grass landscape laid out to keep the milk cow, the horse and the donkey cropping or grazing. The path to the house is lined with clean conch shells and carpeted with white sand. The outside of the house is white-washed with home-made white lime, made by burning lime kiln—this is what makes the walls of the house in the first place. It is called wattle and daub. A wooden door is spaced in the centre of the front side with a window on either side of the door, also made of wood, and airtight when closed. There's a simple little drawstring curtain across the window space, shimmering with the cool breeze blowing against it. The locks on both door and windows are likely to be only bits of line tied to a nail on either end—the old folks guarded only against the weather, never against robbers.

"Come in! Come in!" we are greeted, although we are not even known in our identity, but the housewife is in no way embarrassed to invite us in. This is her palace, and she is proud of it. The seatings are a couple of homemade benches to seat two people, or, in more fortunate cases, a few wood chairs originally salvaged from wrecks, but they will last a lifetime and beyond. Now that we are inside and seated, our eyes can rove around and register for us the inside layout. We are seated in what is called the hall, or sometimes, the drawing-room. The large table standing in the centre, made of either cedar or mahogany and covered with a lace table cloth, is not a dining table. That table no doubt bears all of the family's choice wares, drinking glasses of cut glass, antique bowls and china dishes. There are no closets nor cabinets, so the treasures are openly displayed, but even the toddlers are taught not to touch that table.

Now just look down at that floor you are standing on. That looks too good to walk on. Every weekend the housewife is on her knees scrubbing those pine boards. What does she use to make it so clean without the aid of modern detergents? Her main tool was a piece of fish hide or a half of a "he coconut'—that is, a coconut that formed no nut inside. This, along with some soapy water or some lye made from ashes out of the fireside, served as a cleaning solution. The floor is set with 1 x 12 pine boards and really looks good after being cleaned.

Depending on how many girls are in the family, there are perhaps three or more bedrooms in the house, small but clean. In each room we see a homemade wooden bed stead. The beds and pillows are sacks sewn to the required size, made of sail cloth, or what was called 'ducking'. The sacks have been stuffed with dry banana trash. The master bed is a large four-poster frame, much bigger than all the other beds in the house. No, there are no bathrooms inside. Each family member gets his/her bath in a large, zinc bath-pan, usually in the kitchen. Then somewhere in the back of the yard you will find an outdoor privy that serves as the toilet.

The home's dinner table is likely to be homemade of local mahogany and large enough to seat six or more people. If chairs are at the table they are likely to be of shipwreck origin; not pretty, but strongly made. Over there in the corner is a built-in food locker where all the groceries are kept. They don't have a variety of cans and packages like we have today, but they do have food to eat daily. On the top of the locker are the crockery wares that are used on a day-to-day basis. There is no running water anywhere. The water is kept in a covered bucket. Don't expect to get a drink of ice water on this visit. When you are offered a glass of lemonade, as most certainly you will be, it will only be room temperature, but given from a free, loving heart; or you might even be offered a cup of coffee spiced with fresh cow's milk or coconut milk.

The kitchen is a separate structure away from the house. There is no gas, oil, or electric stove. All the food is cooked on a caboose, or a fire hearth, with firewood for fuel. This is a very smoky procedure, which no doubt is the great reason why this kitchen is built away from the house. The main meal of the day is served some time in the afternoon, and it is usually a one-pot affair, called a "rundown". This has come to be Cayman's unofficial national dish. For the curious ones who are interested in how and of what the meal is created, it is fitting that I should enshrine the recipe right here for future generations.

CAYMAN RUNDOWN

Ingredients: A couple of dry coconuts; some local ground provisions, such as cassava, yam, sweet potato and changed plantains; fish, salted or fresh, or salt beef; onion, celery and green peppers; a few tablespoons of flour.

Procedure: If using salt beef, remember the meat must be tendered and desalted in advance. If using fresh fish, wash it well with limes or vinegar, and season with seasoned-salt and black pepper combined, then place minced onions and celery and green pepper into scorches (scoring) in the fish. Set it aside for a couple of hours to absorb the seasoning and relish. Chip and blend the coconuts, and wash out the trash straining out the pure white milk. Set the coconut milk to boil in a pot different from the one intended for the dinner. In the cooking pot, drop a spoonful or two of butter and let melt to a golden brown. Add two tablespoons of flour, depending on the amount of gravy you will be needing. Stir the flour into the hot butter sauce and pour in the hot coconut milk and stir to give the mixture a body. Into the boiling broth carefully place your provisions that have been peeled, washed and cut in serving pieces. Lastly put the pieces of seasoned fish or salt beef on top of everything, and cover the pot to cook under medium fire. When the provision is cooked the fish will be too, and your rundown will be ready to serve. Corn meal or flour dumplings may also be cooked on the top of the fish if desired—the old folks liked dumplings in their brew. This is a delicious meal when well prepared. So we have finished our tour of the old time Caymanian home with which arrangement the residents were happy and contented.

The family life of old was built on a foundation of love. They vowed for better or for worse, until separated by death, and to that they clung. In most instances they reared large families—10 or 12 children being a common trend among them—and the wife was content with what the husband brought home. What have we got today? Hasn't family life become a mockery in society in this present age? So few marriages seem to be withstanding the tests of life for a lifetime; we wonder where is the example the forefathers left us? Marriages seem like a big movie play now. We build big beautiful houses and buy expensive cars holding high paying jobs while true marital love goes in hiding.

In contrast to what we saw of yesterday, just take a look inside one of those $300,000 houses of today with all the modern luxuries money can buy. They have the most fancy bedroom sets to sleep with. There living-room is elegant; the kitchen looks just like a magazine show piece. Their bathrooms, two or three to a house, are fabulous. Television sets are all over the place, while chandeliers glisten from the ceilings. Here though, is where we apply the brakes. This is no doubt as far as happiness reaches. The house, in all its splendours, is hardly theirs at all; they work long and hard hours just to pay the mortgage on the house and car; they have little or no time for family life together; they are grouchy and irritated with each other; the children are neglected, and Dad takes to spending long hours in bars. Fights ensue and life somehow becomes unbearable for the couple. Soon a divorce decree is granted; another family life is shattered.

History shows that the Cayman Islands survived over the first half of the 20th century on rope-making as the only localized industry that existed. Men went to sea, caught turtles and such like, but that of course was a trade and not an industry. The turtles were caught most often in Nicaragua with a tax being paid to the Nicaraguan Government on each head caught. The rope industry was carried on in all of the three Islands and was maintained primarily by women. However in many instances whole families were involved in the process since, for many, rope was their source of survival.

Turning out a coil of rope was not an easy task since it all had to be done manually and the hard way. A length of finished rope was expected to be 25 fathoms. Grand Cayman was specially blessed with thatch trees, as the old folks called them, used to make the rope. The first step was always a hard one—collecting the tops from the interior. This was done under dire circumstances the most of the time; cliffs and swamps had to be reckoned with, and long distances covered, fighting armies of mosquitoes just to find the tops and cut them. Care had to be taken not to damage the tree because in another month's time another leaf would be ready for cutting. The same trees were farmed for years except for fire destroying them. The tops cutters usually went on Mondays in parties of twos and threes to gather the week's supply. They had to travel three or more miles into the interior to find the good buds. One person would cut 200 or more for that day and tie them together by twos, leaving them to dry until the next week and picking up those that were drying from the week before to take home. The dried leaves were much lighter to carry and were ready for instant use. The first effort was to behead the tops and strip them into strings.

Quite often the women sat up late at nights to weave sufficient strands to make the rope the next morning; it took about 30 tops to make a length of rope. Making the rope was the last step and sometimes a troublesome one. The strand was stretched out in three lengths of about 30 fathoms. Each strand was attached to a winch with three handles on one end and with a single handle, called a cart, on the other end. The person who turned that handle controlled how fast the rope was made, while the winch controlled the texture of the rope—hard laid, or soft. There was also a third person in the process, the one who handled the cob—a round piece of wood with holes in it—that united the strands in one single line. Next, the finished product had to be trimmed, coiled, and securely lashed for shipping. The whole purpose of the hard work placed on the making of the rope was now achieved when off to the shop it was sent to exchange for the necessities of the day. Throughout the Islands there were little stores scattered around whose trade and business depended largely on exchanging their wares for these ropes. They, in turn, sent the ropes to Jamaica to exchange for goods.

Cash sales were small in the Islands in those days. H. O. Merren and Company had businesses going all over in every district. Next to the Merrens was Dr. Roy McTaggart, although he never branched out as did the Merrens. From Island-wide, people went to George Town to shop but particularly at around Christmas. About the first week in December, from the countrysides they went, by boat, or horseback, or even walking, to spend the four or five pounds in cash they had scraped and saved to buy clothes for the family.

Up until the mid-1930s, there was no automotive transportation from East End and North Side. Because there were no ready-to-wear clothes being sold, the housewife bought cloth by the yard and did her own sewing for the entire family, both males and females. The art of tailoring was early passed on to young girls by their mothers, and the general responsibilities of life were pressed into the young ladies' minds at an early age in preparation for womanhood. When they came to the wedded time of life they already knew all that Mama knew before them. This no doubt was the first great reason why old-time marriages lasted out their contracts. The couple began life together in a responsible manner. Young men and young women alike were prepared for the demands of life.

Young people coming out of school had no jobs to go to. There was but a small incentive for one to obtain an education beyond being able to read and write in a fashion. In fact, real education could not be obtained in the Cayman Islands 60 years ago and backwards. The Jamaica Local, up to Third Year, was available for a special class of people—those who could afford the cost. My personal school equipment, over a period of two years in private school and seven years in public school, consisted of a slate, a reading book, and just one exercise book at a time. A slate pencil was cut in half and one part carried to school until it was used up.

A lead pencil was used right down to the eraser.

Many children of my childhood went to school without hearing a word called breakfast. Lunch had to be a very simple fare. The big meal of the day was mostly late in the afternoon and consisted of a plate of the old Cayman rundown as described earlier. However, that meal seems to have contained a lot of energy-providing protein. There was no other source of strength anywhere other than the type of foods that were eaten, yet it's a fact that the old-time people had more strength and energy than can be found anywhere today. In fact I may say there were some giants in the land in old times. They came up the hard way, conditioned to hardships. I once asked a man of about 300 pounds what he ate when he was growing up. Here is what he said, "My boy when I was a child and older, I had a tin cup of bush tea sweetened with cane juice or syrup, with a roast plantain or sweet potato, or a piece of cassava bammy and fried fish for breakfast. Later, about mid day, if I wanted to, I chopped a coconut or two for lunch; then late afternoon I ate my plate of boil up." This man was a huge character with uncommon strength. He lived to be 88 years of age, and died a natural death of old age. He lived on the fat of the land and the sea all his life. Most assuredly there's lots of virtue in seafoods.

As a boy I lived with very little but not on the side of want and poverty. I did not have to endure hunger and privation the way many of my friends did. My grandfather always seemed to have enough and some to spare of the things that were available in his days. Grandpa reared hogs in goodly numbers and kept large tracts of cultivations. He had many fruit trees of varied kinds. He was a painter and artist, as well as a stone-wall layer. My father was a seaman, a top cook of his day. He was constantly at sea, and when he returned home one might think he was about to open a small grocery store. Still, I did not grow up being fed with a silver spoon. I always worked before I was big enough to work, but I had no experience of going to bed hungry because there was nothing to eat, as was the lot of some of us. Many of my friends could often call me blessed because I so often spared them the agony of going to sleep hungry because I had something to spare. Idleness was never a part of my life. I had no time to get myself in trouble because there was always something to do. Did the Prodigal Son in the Bible think he had problems with hogs?

Well, he should ask me something. I fed hogs mornings and evenings until my grandfather couldn't have them anymore. Then I turned to cows. Now I keep on asking myself, which do I hate most? Cows or hogs? That of course could be counted into a part of old-time industries—growing hogs and cows, the same as cultivating.

Looking backward into the past, I see the Cayman Islands in three phases of life. During my early childhood, the country lay helplessly dormant even as a newborn baby with no way of getting itself out of its helpless condition. We had nothing and knew not how to get anything aside from the bare little necessities for a humble existence. If we were hungry, we looked to the sea to satisfy that hunger. The sea, combined with the soil, plus the mercies of a loving God, served to sustain the old-time Caymanians.

But let's not cherish the idea that they had nothing to do to survive. No, life in the old time was hectic. Whatever the tasks might have been that became necessary to perform they had to be accomplished by bare muscular strength. They built whole houses with a hammer, a square and a hand saw. Some were fortunate enough to have a hand plane, but the most popular tool for trimming and dressing was a machete, or perhaps a hatchet. They shaped their own dug-out canoes from large cedar trees. How very beautiful some of those canoes were. My own grandfather had one as a heritage from his father dating back to the late 18th century. He surely prided that cedar canoe. The old-timers knew nothing about motors, inboard or outboard; they depended on the wind in their sails or on paddles to get them where they wanted to go.

It is true history that at one time men from Grand Cayman worked in Little Cayman in the phosphate industry, and that they commuted by canoes between the two Islands. They left East End or North Side on Sunday evening, weather permitting, and sailed or rowed their craft through the night to be at work Monday morning. On Friday afternoon they set sail again in the trade wind to spend the weekend at home. During those days, Little Cayman was an industry centre. However, because of the many devastating storms that so often blew over the Island, homes and businesses were destroyed from time to time. The old salts having died out, the younger ones were now out seeking greener pastures, and who can blame them?

65

In Grand Cayman during that first phase of existence there were not that many people who were able to claim permanent residence here, and so primarily it was the few who remained to carve something out of nothing for the many who would afterward plant their feet on these rocks. I asked an old-timer years ago, "Why do you think your forefathers stuck with all the hardships in Grand Cayman?" He said, "Because this was the one place in the world they could find peace with no wars to fight." A good enough reason, I would dare say. It's marvellous that we, so far down the road in time from those early settlers, can still say, "It's peaceful here." Not too many civilized countries of our age can boast the same.

The second stage of progress saw us haltingly taking a step at a time, reaching out after improvements, during the years of World War II. It was then, for the first time, that many Caymanian families were able to shed their primitive styles of life for a little more modern experience, even as coming out of diapers and stepping into shorts. Up until the early '40s, the ways of living had been the same as in the early part of the century, but the great shot in the arm was given when our men volunteered to serve in the various sections of defence during those terrible war days, and the mail began to carry cheques each month to individual families. Mail service to the Islands had been quite an unbearable situation. Only perhaps once each month, after the introduction of the *M. V. Cimboco,* it came, but previous to that it was carried by schooners that sailed unscheduled or, may I say, when it was convenient. Post Offices around the world did not know anything about a place called Cayman Islands. In fact, even in the '50s and '60s I have been to postal agencies where no one ever heard of Grand Cayman. I remember specially once trying to register a letter in Cape Town, South Africa, to Grand Cayman which was a real trying, difficult affair. They insisted that it was Jamaica, but finally I got them to accept a via-Miami transit. That letter finally did reach my father about three months afterward.

The Cayman Islands having for 100 years or more been a dependency of Jamaica, only received, as it were, the crumbs from the master's table. However, the islands that time forgot, by no coincidence, did have some sensible, intelligent men, even if they were uneducated, for such times as when they were needed most—men such as Dr Roy McTaggart and others with him who could look into the future and determine what was best for their country's good—and as soon as the Islands set themselves adrift from Jamaica things began to happen fast and sure. It is satisfying to say that the movements of the '60s and '70s served to establish today's Cayman. There is where we can see good growing into better, and better evolving into best. The form of government changed from a selection of vestrymen and justices to elective legislators, and we owe a deep appreciation to them for having laid the foundation of development on which succeeding Governments have only built.

Some people will tell us that the new Cayman was born of tourism. I say "No, a thousand times no." It was seamen, thanks to National Bulk Carriers of New York, who set the islands on a progressive movement. The seamen first started the building programme. They first started the importation of motor vehicles, making motor cars more common than donkeys and horses were in the old times. The seamen started all of their development when there were no banks to borrow from. When my house was being built I spent more than two years on a ship without a vacation, but when I came home and spent that first night in it, I felt like a king sitting on his own throne. Before I went to bed that night I went to see the contractor and paid him the very last penny for the house; boy what a feeling! No bank mortgage, no hardware bills to pay. I had years before bought the land on which the house stood and a large area of land around it. I take pleasure, like many other men, in saying, "I own a piece of Grand Cayman because I bought it." In case some people may be thinking that all Caymanians own was handed to them by tourism, I must emphasize the fact that Cayman started her upward trend because of men who were not afraid to risk their lives in the perils of the many waters in the oceans of the world.

We endured hurricanes, typhoons, fires, and sinking ships.

We went into below-freezing weathers and snowstorms.

We baked in Persian Gulf summer heat.

But we did it all for a better Cayman than that which our fathers had known. Truly it can be said that they that go down to the sea in ships, that do business in great waters, these see the goodness of the Lord and His wonders in the deep.

8

THE
RISE
BEGINS

Sybil, my wonderful lady from George Town, became my wife in 1965, and I spent three months at home with her before returning to ships and the sea; this time to Brazil and the Persian Gulf, making even letters difficult passing between us. But even that was near home when compared with having changed charter in mid-term to Japan and Kuwait. Well, I stayed out there for 18 months, day and date, Sunday 18 October to Sunday 18 May, before returning home. It was then that my darling wife laid down the ultimatum for me: If I am your wife then you stay with me; if you are married to ships then go back home. Well, for the first period of my whole life I had no desire to return to sea. I had been accustomed to four or five weeks at home, and then like a fish on dry land I yearned to be back out there quickly. In other words, the sea was my home, and Cayman was a nice spot to visit once in a while for a short period. I wondered at first how I would live up to my wife's demands, but it didn't take me long to know that indeed I was married to Sybil Harris and not ships.

By the middle and late '60s the Cayman Islands were jogging along fairly well. The infancy and crawler stages were of the past. Progress was marked on every milepost up the road. Barclays Bank had by now established itself in George Town while a few other companies were setting up housekeeping. Tourists were dropping down out of the skies weekly in small numbers while LACSA and BWIA planes made regular stops at the Owen Roberts airport. Every few dollars served the purpose of helping build the economy. By then we had taken a leave of absence from Jamaica and were testing out internal self-government; a form of government which is still in operation. The battle was in full array against our fierce ever-present enemies, the mosquitoes; soon they were being controlled, although never then or ever will they be eradicated.

Soon investors began to see Grand Cayman as a safe place to spend their money. Hotels began to grace the landscape on the western beach. There were all types of businesses springing up, as it were, overnight, and hardware soon became a big thing due to the many construction projects that started blossoming over the Island.

Once upon a time, when we were still crawling, Owen Roberts airport was built in a very simplified way but enough to allow LACSA's prop planes to land and take off. The terminal was like something out of the jungle, but it served well its purpose; because of that giant stride forward, seamen had no difficulties in find conveyance from home to ship, and then back home. Caymanian seamen flew worldwide to join the ships of National Bulk Carriers. Many young seamen saw it all only as a continuous funfare, without a thought to the disastrous spending of their dollars, but the majority of men were dead serious about their savings. By the late '60s many Caymanian seamen, like myself, who were family men, had decided to give home life a chance to work for them. There were many jobs opening up over the land, moreso in the construction business, as well as in the hotel industry.

Having worked as a Chief Steward for many years, it was not hard for me to obtain a job as Chief Cook at the Pageant Beach Hotel for a season. However, even though I loved to cook and knew something about the job, hotel work never appealed to me. When that first season was over, I took a job with Kel's Farm Supplies—one of Mr. Norberg Thompson's early ventures, along with the Wholesome Bakery. Jobs had become easier to get—my wife spent the major part of her working days in the employment of H. O. Merren who were then the ruling business magnates in the Island along with R. E. McTaggart—and I next took a supermarket job in the Merrens' employ. This was not the type of supermarket we know today, but it did well for those times. The Merrens supplied the Island wholesale, and had a retail branch in each district in Grand Cayman. A lot of people had known me from Kel's Farm, and so it did not take me long to become popular with the community at Merrens. People Island-wide shopped there even as in today's Foster's and Kirk's. The Byrite Supermarket soon came into being and likewise the Kirk Plaza, but

Merren's still held their own, and I enjoyed working there, but there always seemed to be a broader field for improvements in one's life in those developing days, and I soon made a change.

Having buried my dear father on 6 January 1970, the very next day I took up work selling insurance for the First Federation Insurance Company of Clearwater, Florida. We did health insurance primarily, with life thrown in as optional. Due to my popularity at Merren's for three years, in my first year as an insurance agent I became the top agent in the entire West Indies—the company had established business in every Caribbean Island including Haiti. In that first year I won a trip to Bogota, Columbia to an insurance conference that was held there. I was then champion, but I did not rest on that achievement; by the end of my second year I had become an ace, by which I could take my wife, expense-free to Luxembourg. What a trip that was as we attended that convention there. We went into the scene of the Battle of the Bulge. We toured the huge American cemetery. We travelled a whole day into Germany, and saw many other great attractions, all for free.

Back in the Cayman field, things were getting better all the time. More and more money was in the reach of the public, and more and more people were being convinced of the need for insurance. Thus my third year was even better than those before, and now the convention venue was London, England which was another one of the many honeymoons my wife and I had not enjoyed before.

Truly those insurance days were the crowning ones of my whole life. I did not attend the fourth year convention in Puerto Rico for one reason or another; I just accepted my bonus with a big smile. Then of course, as with all good things, there had to be a changing point. The owner of that company died, and his wife sold out to another company who soon enough played the part of some insurance people who make sweet, heavenly promises verbally, hoping that nobody takes the time to read the fine print of the policy. For me, insurance became very fraudulent and a state of affairs in which I would have no part, therefore I withdrew. So once again I was back with H. O. Merren. By this time they were operating the brand-new beautiful complex down north. By then Cayman was moving ahead at a full gallop; no stopping her progress at all. From our modest beginnings, we had reached world recognition. Expatriates

71

from all over were moving in ... people of all trades and professions ... there was a place for all of them in Grand Cayman. The great task of building Cayman was in action. A new modern supermarket, Kirk Plaza, dominated the scene in the centre of town and beckoned all to come and enjoy low prices and efficient services, with convenient parking. Thus the Merrens' position declined in the competitive world, possibly moreso due to their out-of-town location. Within a few months, my employment had to be terminated.

■

My hunt for another job immediately started; not that I was broke, or down and out, but at 50 years of age who wants to spend his life's savings to live from? But one thing was against me in getting the kind of job I wanted: I was a Seventh Day Adventist and would not work on Saturdays. That was the reason the lot fell first on me to be laid off at Merren. The day was against me in the eyes of would be employers, but my God wasn't against me. I owned a little building in East End that once served as a cook shop, run by my father while he was able. It was now mine and built on a choice piece of land which had been a heritage from my dear mother. I had some money in Jamaica which Mr. Manley's government would not allow me to take out of the country, and after consultation with my wife and the Lord we decided to start our own little retail store and use the money in Jamaica to buy goods. Our little place was equipped with shelves and counters, and it was stocked tightly. However, there was no encouragement coming from the community for such a "stupid venture". Already there were three long-standing stores in the district, among them the H. O. Merren & Co. branch looking right into my front door. A few hundred yards away was Mr. W. W. Conolly, an established business long before I was born. Just down the road was Mr. Thomas Rankine, there longer than I could remember. So the people were right in thinking and saying my venture scarcely was worth a burlap sugar bag, especially that I would be closing Friday nights and Saturdays. I could not be discouraged by anyone. I just threw myself into business even as though I were the manager of a modern supermarket. I pushed for success. Even my wife did not have faith in what I was doing. She continued in her job as an insurance secretary, but before long she saw my rapid success which could be nothing short of a miracle. She moved in with me whole-heartedly, and together we moved on. We had been there less than two years when the Merren's branch store closed up and who would believe it! Will and Sybil bought the Merren's local business! Our store, Will and Sybil's Little Economy, was moving ahead. However, we must render thanks and appreciation to the Barclays Bank for kind assistance all the way through, and above all to the Creator for blessing us. For economical reasons we soon merged the Merren's store into our original, giving us a general store. At one stage we employed three people along with us to operate the business. Surely God honors those who honor Him.

During the 1970s, I was also chosen by Government as an aide to Mr. Sleep, the adjudicator of lands and survey for the cadastral survey. That was not a very rewarding task as far as public opinions were concerned. People had centuries of land disputes, and many were unhappy and critical of the tribunal's decisions. If ever a rift came in old-time family relationships it just had to be concerning lands, and that situation lingers on today among Caymanians. There have been some very serious events in times past over land ownership. Before the cadastral business was complete I was honored by being appointed a Justice of the Peace, an appointment that I honor much. Shortly after that I was made a Marriage Officer and officiated at many marriages with locals and foreigners. I served the Protection Board, the Planning Board, the Water Authority, the Stamp Committee, and the Prison Inspectorate, and I more recently served four years on the Adoption Board. My first ambition is to serve the God I love and, secondly, my beloved country.

I greatly love humanity, and am bound over to do all the good I can, to whomever I can, whenever I can, and as one witnesses the day-to-day happenings around our beautiful homeland the heart must often be saddened by what is seen among our once lovely young people who so often fail society's high expectation of them. Undoubtedly there are pressures and distractions these days we never dreamed of, but the unanswered question remains to be answered: where is society heading? Past generations knew nothing about such substances as those that contaminate our youth today. Well, I guess neither did I know about such

The Mail Lady

things as rapes and robberies, or burglaries while growing up. Without a doubt, my childhood days in the Cayman Islands were as close to Heaven as one will experience this side of the Kingdom.

All during my boyhood days, up until the early '30s, there was no police force as such in these Islands. Each district had a district constable who in most cases doubled as the mail carrier and peace-keeper. He also organized search parties for fugitives and lost people, as sometimes happened.

Let's take a look at the mail service back then. In previous years, there was an individual woman, Mrs. Jenetta Wood, who walked twice per week from East End to George Town and back carrying the mail each way; that along with whatever packages were requested of her to carry per favour. She would leave East End about two o'clock in the morning— what the old folks called "first cock crow"—and she would get to George Town around nine or ten o'clock when businesses were open. She would go over to the old courthouse, deliver the mail, and then she would have a little rest. Around two in the afternoon, she would pick up the East End mail and head back, getting home around nine at night. At that time, there was a kind of horse track from George Town to Bodden Town but past that, really nothing. Between Bodden Town and Breakers she would have to walk the beach, then there was one little footpath through Breakers to Frank Sound. From there she would have to get back on the beach and walk to Cottage, then you hit another little footpath through the woods. She did this twice a week; I believe she was getting paid 10 shillings a month for that. I knew the old lady personally. She lived to be one 102 years of age.

By the mid-1920s, however, the district constables had been organized into the mail service. Three of them operated between Bodden Town, East End and North Side. There was an old lady who lived right abreast of North Side Road at Frank Sound She lived there alone, and her kitchen was used as a mail exchange centre. There was where East End, North Side and Bodden Town met three times per week with mails.

Mrs. Tama Johnson's place was also a resting place for travellers walking between the three districts. In those days, the beach was the only roadway from Pease Bay east, so people walking the route, which could be a daily affair, could stop and rest themselves and have a cool drink of water from Mrs. Johnson's well. There was no human habitation between Frank Sound and East End or between there and Old Man Bay. The journey to Old Man Bay was a hazardous one. There were many swamps to wade through when rain fell—which was regular in the old days—and there were many gates to open and close because of cow pastures along the way.

In spite of such conditions, Mr. Tydeman Ebanks fulfilled his weekly duties for many years, riding his donkey through water, sun hot, or swarms of mosquitoes, until the middle of the '30s when motor vehicles were able to make the crossing. The road, if you can call it that, through Frank Sound land was just a track, but it was a great blessing to the residents of the northern District, even as the opened path to East End was to East Enders.

But let's talk a little more about the mail service. Foreign mail reached George Town perhaps once a month from Jamaica in the old days, carried by schooners and later by the *M. V. Cimboco*. It was then sorted there in the imitation post office which was situated downstairs in the old Court House. (That building now houses our National Museum.) Then it took the slow journey over land to the several destinations. Each district had a mail distribution centre. The districts' JPs back then had a lot of power in their hands. They acted as postmasters, magistrates, legislators and, in some cases, customs and immigration officers. East End was a port of entry until the 1940s. Mr. Austin Conolly could rightly be called a Mayor in East End and so could Mr. Louie Chisholm in North Side as well as Mr. Logan Bodden in Bodden Town.

Schooners coming from Jamaica stopped at East End to unload the freight for that district for the many little merchants who operated there. Later, when the *Cimboco* came into being she was the certified mail carrier, freight and passenger boat between Jamaica and the Cayman Islands. She stopped at Cayman Brac first on the down run and lastly on the Jamaica route. When she came to Grand Cayman, East End was the first stop.

When the Honourable A. W. Cardinall came to the Cayman Islands as the Commissioner, he received a cannon salute from the East Enders. That, he later said, had scared him to his wit's end, and from then on he always had a special liking for East Enders all the years he spent here.

There never was a more patriotic people anywhere than the old East Enders. They were always ready to do a fist fight to maintain the honour of the Crown, and the date 24 May, Queen Victoria's birthday, was almost held sacredly among them. King George V was the most special of all humans in those days. Mr. A. W. Cardinall also won a very special spot in the hearts of East Enders and North Siders when, a short time after taking office in the Islands, he opened a vehicular road through from Bodden Town to East End and North Side. This was indeed the greatest gift ever given to a people up until that time. Many were the lives that might have been spared a while longer had it not been so difficult to reach medical aid. The residents were then privileged to ride to town whether for shopping or medical purposes. Before that, if you wanted to go to George Town from East End, like the lady who delivered the mail, you had to go on horseback or walk. There were some big canoes that would bring goods up from George Town, but bad weather would stall them. Also it wasn't easy, because you could sail down but coming back was usually four or five men pulling on big oars. People today find it hard to believe, but there were many grown people in East End who had never seen George Town—there were hundreds of people who lived and died in those districts and never came out—so the opening of the car road was a major change in the way people lived.

Another strong remembrance of Mr. Cardinall stands out in every district of Grand Cayman in the form of the town halls he had built. Then there are the impressive Post Office and the Library in George Town. These buildings all served many purposes in times past, and are all kept today in decent repairs. Could Mr. Cardinall return today and take a walk around town he would be rather bewildered in finding locations. Cardinall Avenue, named after him, is a very busy tourist centre with all the freeport stores and banks gracing the scene. Even the old market has been changed to a modern use and looks.

Just as the motor vehicles have brought an end to horse and mule days, even so Caymanians now travel to the U.S.A. in a much easier form than they used to get from one point to the other of the Island. Schooners and even motor vessels of the long ago that were used for travel have now disappeared from the scene, and one can fly to Miami, Florida several times per day. One can have his fish-and-chips lunch in London, and enjoy prime ribs or T-bone steaks in Grand Cayman. There is a direct air link between England and Grand Cayman. No longer do we see white canvas flapping in the wind, with beautiful white hulls swinging on their moorings in George Town harbour in the light shifting winds. Today we are looking at streamlined passenger ships, sometimes as many as four at one time, along with flashy yachts owned by the very rich of the outside world living on board their own luxurious, little hotels. What great changes time has brought about in these once little-known, forgotten Islands! Truly have the old folks said, "time changes things". We live in a changed and changing world, and it is no marvel that the Cayman Islands have changed along with the world. However, one may not conclude that all the changes taking place have been, or are being the very best thing that could happen to Caymanians. The living standards are said to be very high, but it is not logic to say that all Caymanians feed from the tree of life; there are still a great many who endure but a meagre existence. There are still far too many gathering from the tree of knowledge of good and evil, and, as it were, finding the evil sweeter. Many, of course, set their own pace for living. Well, when one chooses to live in the gutter he can enjoy only what the gutter offers.

9

MYSTERY
AND
TRAGEDY

Today we see many couples who have lived together for a quarter of a century or more, reared children and have become grandparents, and then suddenly we hear they are divorcing, or already divorced. It is a proved fact that fabulous houses, beautiful cars, and lots of money do not create happiness. Love is still the only ingredient that lays the foundation for a happy and lasting union between a man and a woman, and though the old folks had but little together they loved much. The family relationship used to be a sacred as religion.

I now bring to the attention of my readers a most sensational love story worthy of being immortalized in the historic archives of the Cayman Islands for the use of future generations. I term this true story, "Love Unending".

In the late 1900s, there lives in a certain area of Grand Cayman a colored family known by the name of Welcome. No one seems to have known under what circumstances old Jack Welcome happened to reach the north-east coast of Grand Cayman, a totally unsettled area, except that he must have been a shipwreck survivor. Suffice it to say, Jack is of African descent, he has a wife with him, and he enters into a large tract of unclaimed property with miles of beach and interior lands which he soon lays claim to, establishing boundaries as he chooses. He builds a house, probably from shipwreck lumber, just east of where Morritt's Tortuga now exists, and in process of time Jack's wife bears him three sons like the sons of a giant. Abner is the eldest, Tyler the second, and Thomas the youngest. They are boys of stature and strength. Their father teaches them the art of boat building, and they start putting together boats from the remains of wrecks. Old Jack is also a navigator which knowledge he passes on to his sons, and soon Abner is mastering his own yawl in the turtle-fishing trade. The boys quickly discover there is a better life awaiting them off shore, away from Colliers, so Abner and Tyler take up residence in Nicaragua, acquiring much property on the main land and in Corn Island where they do very well for themselves.

Thomas, with a strong love of the soil, remains to help his aged father in farming and cattle rearing, but, when the old man passes away, young Tom loses interest in farming. One day, having boarded a whaling ship to sell hogs and provisions, as the natives customarily do with passing ships, no doubt due to his great stature and strong appearance he is hired as a deck hand. For more than eight years, Tom remains onboard that whaler before it once again passes by close enough to Grand Cayman to set him safely ashore in East End. Thomas Welcome is now the richest man in the eastern district; he said there had been much money in catching whales.

He buys a large tract of front land in the centre of East End and builds the largest lumber house to be seen in the area. This is not a thatch house such as the times offered. It is a five-bed-room, shingled-roof house. Tom's next move is to search for a life-long companion, a wife to have and to hold for true love's sake, and he finds the type of woman he is searching for at Northward, Bodden Town. Matilda Wood is a beautiful woman in her late twenties. She is on the white side by appearance, but Thomas Welcome, though dark-skinned, is a handsome, respectable man of East End. He has money and lots of property, along with his own nice house of the times, so Josiah Wood does not have to fast and pray to reach a decision to give his daughter's hand in marriage to this fine gentleman. The love between Thomas and Matilda later becomes proverbial, and in time they become the happy parents of three sons and three daughters— Boyd, Ronald and Barrett are the sons; Ivy, Miriam and Lydia are the daughters.

As this particular part of the story begins, Tom is engaged once again in farming and cattle rearing as he had done in his youthful days, and at which he is an expert. His lands are on the other side of the Island, and, because of the inconvenience of travelling on a daily basis between his home and the farm six miles away, the inseparable couple build a little house on the farm where they usually stay from Monday until Friday each week, unless something is beyond their control.

That fateful Sunday morning, Uncle Tom and Aunt Tilly are in their seats in the Presbyterian Church. The year is 1930. It has been a good year for produce. There has been lots or rain throughout the year, the corn crops have been great, and everything is flourishing. Even now, in December the rains are still falling heavily. Over the weekend and into Monday there has been bad weather, so the couple remain grounded at home through Monday. By Tuesday morning the rains have ceased, and thus they saddle their horses and set off for the farm where they plan to remain until Friday. Uncle Tom is now past 70 years of age, an old man of his time, but robust, strong and full of action and ambition. He has three special loves: first the Lord he relies on, then his wife who is the pride of his life and his joy of living, and thirdly the soil which he often said is near to his heart because of that he had been made.

On Tuesday morning 9 December 1930, Uncle Tom and Aunt Tilly set off for the farm to do together the many chores they have been doing for several years routinely—to plant things, to see them grow, and to protect them from predators, whether weeds or animals. Right now, with Christmas approaching, they hardly know what to reap first; there is so much produce just ready for reaping. But something goes terribly wrong that day for the couple.

The old man could have gone to one of his pastures attending to his cows—there were two calves borned that week—or perhaps he goes to work in another cultivation away from the house. Well, wherever he has been, when he returns to the house expecting to eat his afternoon meal, his wife is nowhere be found. He sees she has not even lit a fire since having their morning coffee. He goes out into the cultivation shouting at the top his lungs. No amount of yelling and calling her name brings any response from her. The echo of his own voice and the thunder in the distance are all that reach his ears. Beyond that there is silence.

As Uncle Tom goes searching for his beloved, a dark-looking squall is gathering to the east making the surroundings even more dreary. And then the rain begins to fall—a rain that would prevail for the greater part of the remaining days of that week. All of that afternoon and throughout the night the lightning flashes, the thunder rolls, and the rain pours in torrents.

No one knows how long Uncle Tom searches, but when he finally finds his wife, what a discovery!

"Mama!" as he always called her, "Mama, what happened to you?" he must have said.

He shakes her and keeps on talking to her, but she doesn't stir or answer him. Her skull is crushed over both eyes; pints of blood have drained down on the rock alongside of her. Blood, now clotted, fills her ears, nostrils and mouth. Tom's beloved is dead.

The old man is beside himself; grief has benumbed his whole intellect. He knows now his darling wife is dead, and that she died violently.

The couple had often been heard saying that where one died there the other one would die also. The old man can saddle his horse and ride home to report his gruesome discovery, but he does not think of it. There is no leaving his beloved's side, even now in death.

He does not move from that spot.

He does not even go back to the house to get a blanket or a sheet with which to cover the body. Removing his own shirt he covers her as best he can after fixing the body in a state of death. Then he lies down beside her prepared to die with her. No amount of rain, or thunder or lightning can move him from her side.

Aunt Tilly is dead, and Uncle Tom is to die with her.

■

Very early Friday morning, the 12th of December, the baby boy of the family would go to meet Ma and Pa and help them to get home with the week's produce. As a rule this is done by canoe, but on this week the weather does not permit a boat trip to the north-east coast, so Barrett sets off on horseback.

Hear Barrett's own story:

"I left the horses at the foot of the bluff where the other horses were in a little pasture Pa kept just for the horses. I made my way toward the interior where Ma and Pa would be. I was already soaked to my skin with the drizzling rain that had been falling ever since I left East End. A cup of hot coffee or some good warm fresh milk was uppermost in my mind.

But coming to the house I saw no sign that any one had lived there that week. Their food was as they left home with it, and no fire had been lit. It was as if everything had suddenly come to a standstill.

"Well this was the most confusing situation I had ever found myself into in my 18 years of life. Where could Pa and Ma be? This was the only shelter they had anywhere away from home. I called, or rather I shouted, their names all over the place. I yelled for them like I had never extended my voice before, but there was no sound of their replying.

"I started searching for them. I was wet and shivering in the constant rain, while fear filled my whole body. I kept thinking ... where are Pa and Ma? A state of anguish over took me. I soon detected a bad odour in the air and followed into it. O God! No! No, God, this can't be. I must be still asleep and having a nightmare, I thought. 'Please awaken me to a more pleasant reality, God,' I said out loud. But this was no nightmare. What I was thrown into was a living tragedy; the worst reality I would face in a lifetime. There, before my eyes, were my father and my mother, lying together, both dead, and already in a decomposed state.

"I wasn't sure whether I should just lay there and die with them or try to get home to my sisters. I thought of the arsenic Pa kept in the house to kill rats; ah yes, that would be a good way. But then there were my two dear sisters, Ivy and Miriam; they needed a strong shoulder to lean on. I was the man of the house now. My two older brothers were both away in Nicaragua at that time. Ivy was at home. Miriam was working in George Town, and communication with her would be awfully hard from East End.

"There I was, just me alone, fighting a losing battle. I could not leave my precious parents to be eaten by whatever creatures might prey on them, or to rot on the face of the earth out there. I started to make my way out of the land. I took one of the horses and rode him bareback starting on my way home. Six or seven of the longest miles I have ever trodden lay between me and home.

"I bawled the whole way home. Even as people ran out of their houses to ask questions, I answered no one. Pa and Ma were dead, and I wanted to hear nothing from anyone. School was still in session when I reached the schoolhouse, and knowing my two loved nephews, Clifford and Will were there I called out the sad words to them. Mr. Allen ran out to me and helped me down from the horse, at which time I fainted. It was Mr. Allen who bore the news to my sister Ivy, while the good neighbours worked on me. I finally reached home but have no further recollection of that day". End of quote.

News of Barrett's painful discovery spreads like wild fire through the district—Uncle Tom and Aunt Tilly are both dead. Mr. Austin Conolly, the JP, very quickly gets someone to go on the fastest available horse in the district of Bodden Town to contact Mr. Logan Bodden (he owned one of the Islands' few cars at that time) who would in turn relay the message to the officials in George Town and to Miriam who worked there. The news reaches the doctor and other officials that afternoon, but it is not until Saturday mid-morning that they can get to East End after battling a north-easter all the way in an old "sewing machine" motor boat, and even then they are still far away from the tragic scene. All Friday night, men have been working in the construction of two coffins which the officials take along in their launch as they continue their journey to Bluff Bay, and finally, that evening, a funeral service is held in the interior for the late Thomas and Matilda Welcome. The doctor's diagnosis reads:

"Thomas Welcome died of grief and exposure to inclement weather on or about Thursday 11th of December 1930.
Matilda Welcome died on or about Tuesday 9th of December of serious head injuries caused by forceful connections with a blunt instrument, her brain having been exposed through a gaping wound across her forehead."

This would have to be called the Caymanian love story of the century. Nature itself seems to have made preparation for this tragic romance for not far from the death scene was a spot in the rocky cliff, a level spot of deep earth that was just large enough to hold two coffins.

■

For years after the event, the tale behind Aunt Tilly's death remained a mystery, and indeed many are the tragic events that have taken place in Grand Cayman during the 20th century that have remained mysteries.

That, of course, may chiefly be blamed on the inefficiency of police or lack of police service at all to investigate. In old times, convicting a criminal often depended on just how many eyewitnesses could be found to say, "I saw 'John Doe' in action, in the process of committing a crime." Then, too, 50 years ago and beyond, the Islands knew only brothers, sisters, uncles and aunts, plus everybody's cousins. No one was anxious to rat on the other person who was almost always a relative. In those early years, we know of the mysterious disappearances of people who were never seen or heard from. In more recent times we hear of a few people in West Bay who just stepped out of existence. A father and a son in George Town went fishing and never returned home, although their boat was found on the other side of the Island, many miles away from their fishing location. In Bodden Town, two men, separately, and at different times, evaporated on fishing trips—one from a boat, the other on foot along the shore. This is only to name a few unaccounted for lost ones. There were many hidden crimes in our past history that were not too mysterious after all, if only they had been investigated. The number one cause of bloody crimes had their roots in land disputes. It can truly be said that many old-timers would kill for a foot of land, knowing they could get away with it. In fact, there is more than one story of just that happening.

There's a true story concerning two old men who were in deep contention over the ownership of an area of land, something like 50 acres. Old Jim Jackson had spent several days marking this unclaimed land, but on Sundays, while Jackson was in church, or during the days he was fishing, old Gill went and burnt out Jackson's mark from the tree and set his own. Well, one Friday they appeared before the magistrate to have their case settled. The magistrate, like King Solomon, could see only one solution—he ordered them to appear on the land Monday morning for a fist fight to establish ownership. Two witnesses and the magistrate were to be there as referees between the warriors. Early Monday morning all parties concerned were present, and when the sun rose the fight was declared in progress. Sometime during mid-morning they were allowed a rest period, and then in the afternoon they had time to eat their fried fish and Johnny-cake before the battle continued. Just before the sun faded behind the bushes, old Gill dropped on the ground and conceded the land to old Jackson. To this day, the name of that place is Battle Hill.

This story proves to today's generation that lands, the properties we seem to think so little of today, were once most precious to the settlers, our forefathers.

In East End a very tragic case of violence was recorded: An old man by the name of Milburn McLean left home at daybreak on a Saturday morning to go fishing with his nine-year-old grandson. They were in one of the finest canoes the district possessed. The envy of many boat owners, she was a sleek, fast and steady canoe—not a dugout, but a Honduranian-built bottom. The old man named her *Fiddle* and was down right proud of her as his very own. That morning he decided to go up to the north-east coast to fish because the light south wind that was arising left it pond-smooth on that side. Nobody said they saw him going on that route that morning, but later evidences proved that he did go there. Most fishermen that day would have been in the Gun Bay area, so no doubt the old man was alone to the north-east. However, when late afternoon came, and the fisherman did not return home, the family began to be upset, and when evening drew on a search was arranged. All of East End turned out to at least scan the shorelines, but darkness fell fast, and there was no more than kerosene lanterns to light the search way. So the search had to be called off to wait for daylight.

Sunday morning, bright and early, men in boats, and even women on their feet, resumed the search. But this time it did not take long to find the right trail of the missing fisherman. In the Colliers channel the canoe was found—anchored, but bottom up. There was no sign though of either grandfather or grandson. Now the area had to be closely searched for two bodies. Soon there were people waving and shouting to the boatmen: "We have found the boy." Sure enough, there in a deserted little rocky cove was little Jack's body. It had been pricked by black sea urchins from the sole of the feet to the crown of the head.

Now a more diligent search than ever was organised looking for the old man's body. The canoe having been found, the clue was open for solution, but alas there was never a hint of where the body was, inside or outside of the reef, nor yet along the reef.

The reasoning in the various minds was that the canoe had capsized under sail, or that the old man had a heart attack, and the little boy tried to swim ashore and drowned in the effort.

All of these reasons were insensible since the sail was found on the shore, well-rolled and tied. The old man, in case of a heart attack, would have been in the canoe and not have turned it over—it might have taken two or more real strong men to capsize the *Fiddle*. This was a working boat of a good size.

For many years the unanswered questions remained—how had Aunt Tilly died so violently in such a remote place? What happened to the body of Milburn McLean, a man of about 250 pounds weight?

There is a state called dying and death that makes mankind fearful of his past evil deeds, so to try and correct his character to meet his Maker he usually tells those evil hidden secrets of a lifetime as death draws near. In this manner, the truth became known in those two East End's tragedies.

In the case of Uncle Tom and Aunt Tilly, after many years of a tortured conscience, an old man, while looking into an awful eternity, made his deathbed confession to four men standing over him. He revealed that he had been doing some poaching of ground provisions on the Welcome's land and Aunt Tilly had caught him the act. In shame and panic, he had clubbed her to death and fled. As was suspected at the time, upon finding her, poor old Uncle Tom had truly died a death of love in grief and exposure.

In the case of Milburn McLean, the facts that later came out were these: Setting out to go fishing that morning with his grandson, the old man could not find his spreet—that's the pole fishermen used to push their boats along. He came upon three fishermen who had taken his spreet, and in the course of an argument about it one of the men hurled the spreet at the old man. It flew like a spear and landed flush on McLean's chest and killed him. Although it was accidental, the three fishermen panicked. They buried McLean in the sand up in the grape bush, and then they capsized the boat up in the channel to give the appearance of an accident; that way, the young boy drowned. This revelation was made, years after the incident, also in a deathbed confession by one of the men involved. That area became known as Jack's Barcadere, so named because Jack's little body was found there.

From Thatch Roof to Spanish Tile

10

FROM THATCH ROOF
TO SPANISH TILE

From under thatch-roof to Spanish tile; out of white-lime plaster to cement block wall; from living behind stuffy wooden doors and windows to looking out through graceful glass windows and louvre doors; walking away from the old, hard pine floor, lightly treading on ankle-deep carpets and Persian rugs—this is a picture of yesterday's living quarters contrasted against today's luxurious houses.

Very little by way of living conditions remain today as a reminder of yesterday; present-day developments have totally obliterated the beauties of the past. I have been searching recently for just a glimpse of the old Cayman in the things around us or even in the people's daily living, but nowhere can I see a semblance of my boyhood, except deep down in my remembrances. I let my mind wonder back to those good old days when today was the only day thought about—tomorrow was an unknown day. There just seems to have been lots of time for everything. "I would like to be able to help you, but I am sorry, I can't find the time," was a statement never heard. There was always time to help where help was needed. The sick or bereaved, the aged and helpless, these all received love and affection in the community. Neighbours lived like saints together, and close relatives had an unbroken relationship. During those old days when Daddy went to sea on the schooners, or to Central America to work, Mom took over the role of ordering their household and raising her children in the fear of God and respect for their peers.

Do I hear you saying, Mom had nothing to do, so she had lots of time for charity? That statement is not true. In those old days there was everything for dear Mom to accomplish the hard way. She had no mechanical equipment to assist her with any of her daily tasks. In the first place she was likely to have six or more children to take care of and sometimes there were 10 or 12. Those all were reared from birth to maturity without the benefit of all the aids such as today's mothers know. Who was she that had the pleasure of the presence of a helper to assist in her daily routines? That honour was accorded only to the very top class around the Islands. Babies' diapers had to be washed on a daily basis in a wood tub, scrubbed on a wash board, with only a bit of brown soap as detergent. All the water, for whatever use, had to be carried by hand from community wells. Meals were cooked in a wood-burning process, one pot at a time. Floors were scrubbed the hard way, down on the knees. The family clothes had to be washed and ironed on a weekly basis which was quite an undertaking—washing machines and electric irons were still perhaps on the drawing board somewhere—and all of the family's bread, cornbreads or heavy cakes were her responsibility, as well. Above all, with no refrigerators in which to keep food from one day to the next, like so many families do today, every day was a cooking day, and it must also be remembered that many families of old in this country found their financial survival only in rope-making. There was nothing soft or easy in turning out a coil of rope each day to purchase the day's groceries, but it was done and no one grumbled or complained in the process.

However, let's not think that Mom worked so hard while Dad had it easy. He had the responsibility of providing for his family by land or sea, and mostly by both. A cultivation was somewhat of a must to survive. This had to be done by only muscular strength. Either a man sailed to sea for a livelihood or he worked in a foreign country to support his family. Nevertheless, life's demands were but simple alongside today's grand way of living. A roof over one's head, sheltered from the sun, the rains and the mosquitoes was the first great need for a family. That being taken care of, a couple changes of clothing and providing the daily meals were about the only requirements for happiness. Their main source of contentment sprang out of the love they cherished for one another. Partners knew what true love was all about. They placed the greater emphasis on the marital relationship rather than on the material things which cause so much problems today. Aunt Jane was satisfied with what Uncle Joe could give her and the children.

It is pleasant to reflect one's mind from time to time to those good old care-free days. One didn't feel cheap or worthless because Cousin John was driving a late-model motor car, while he himself couldn't afford to have one of any kind. "Oh boy, what a beautiful motor-boat Tim has while here I am rowing my father's old canoe around." There was hardly anything to cause one to envy the other person for, unless, perhaps his beautiful wife—that was perhaps the most prevalent sin of the old days; there were such beautiful girls around then. Of course the grass always looked greener on the other side of the fence. Even though my wife might have been beautiful, yet Jack's wife would almost always seem more attractive to me. So, while poor Jack's out there on one of his schooner trips, I could be secretly dating his wife at home. And mind you, the old folks were stealthy and secretive about their evil deeds. There were no electric lights to expose one's whereabouts at night, and men still love darkness rather than light when their deeds are evil. There were a great many people of old whose daddy wasn't their daddy at all; Mama just wouldn't tell.

■

I have been on this planet for 70-plus years, during which time I have seen good and evil. I have experienced pleasant times and hard times. I have seen Grand Cayman spring forth from nowhere and grow into a most beautiful oak tree. We must pay tribute to those men of far-sighted vision who so guardedly steered the old ship through all the hidden shoals and have converted the old Liberty ship into a beautiful passenger ship—men such as Dr. Roy McTaggart, Mr. Willie Farrington, Mr. Warren Conolly, Mr. Jim Bodden and Mr. Benson Ebanks, just to name a few of the stalwarts who turned Cayman around. Today, we have responsible legislators taking the oversight of running a sound and peaceful country. The Islands that time forgot for thousands of years are now very much alive, and even as we may question some of the things around us this is a far easier place than the Cayman of the smoke-pot days.

Once I recall one ex-navy man saying Cayman had five wonders—"a deaf doctor" (that was Doctor Hortor), "a shell-shocked preacher" (that was Rev. George Hicks), "a black Rose" (that was the pharmacist Dr. Rose), and "a dumb town clock", (that was on the Town Hall).

In a sense, that is a humourous view; in fact, there are many things about those bygone years that many old-timers yearn for. Developments have truly changed things. We have more money with poorer morals. We see better living conditions but crowned with more crimes. Modern customs have murdered old cultures. We witness an age when the love of the mighty dollar has almost obliterated the love of the Almighty God.

Lord, have mercy on Your people and help us to look again to the old paths we once trod, while You continue to bless our beautiful home land!

GLOSSARY

<u>bammy</u> = rustic alternative to bread made with grated cassava root.

<u>boil up</u> = a traditional stew, similar to "rundown" (see below) but without the coconut and therefore considered not in the same class

<u>brew</u> = stew

<u>caboose</u> = hearth for cooking with firewood as fuel, separated from house

<u>changed plantains</u> = plantains just turning ripe or yellow

<u>chopping pastures</u> = cleaning bush with a machete

<u>cow-itch</u> = a wild-growing vine carrying small pods contact with which produces intense itching

<u>cropping</u> = grazing

<u>cultivation</u> = land planted with plantain, yam, cassava, etc.

<u>heart burden</u> = dedicated mission

<u>knuckling match</u> = a fight

<u>rundown</u> = combination of fish, coconut milk, ground provision, and dumplings, simmered into a thick stew.

<u>scorches</u> = slits cut in the flesh of fish or meat to receive seasoning

<u>spreet</u> = long wooden pole to push boat along close to shoreline

<u>striker</u> = wooden stick with a pointed end, used to spear conch

<u>tops</u> = leaves of thatch palm cut to make thatch rope

Sailor, preacher, farmer, and East End store-owner Will Jackson has written extensively of life in early Cayman. Retired in 1997, he enjoys life with his two beloveds—the village of East End and his wife Sybil.